Pathways

Your journey to emotional wellbeing

D1419796

An Hachette UK Company
www.hachette.co.uk

First published in Great Britain in 2021 by Kyle Books,
an imprint of Octopus Publishing Group Limited
Carmelite House
50 Victoria Embankment
London EC4Y 0DZ

ISBN 978 1 91423 917 5

Text copyright 2021 © Samaritans
Design and layout copyright 2021 © Octopus Publishing Group Ltd

Publishing Director: Judith Hannam
Publisher: Joanna Copestick
Editorial Assistant: Zakk Raja
Copy Editor: Tara O'Sullivan
Design: Paul Palmer-Edwards
Production: Lisa Pinnell

A Cataloguing in Publication record for the title is available
from the British Library.

Printed and bound in China

10 9 8 7 6 5 4 3 2 1

Pathways

Katie Colombus

Contents

Therapy, mindfulness and breathing

Hope, habits and boundaries

Self-care

Over to you

Where to seek further support

Introduction

With all the noise and activity of daily life, it can be difficult to keep up with social demands, money worries, work problems, family issues, relationship dramas, the pressure of unrealistic beauty ideals, caring for others, planning for the future... sometimes we get by, but sometimes we get out of balance. When that happens, our emotions tend to suffer. It's important to recognise when we're off-kilter, because when negative feelings go unchecked, things can start to get worse and sometimes even escalate into distress.

Recent world events have been overwhelming and unsettling, which is why now more than ever it's important to take the time to check in with ourselves, to realise what's going on in our minds and to be curious about why we think and feel the way we do.

Emotional health is just as important as physical health. It affects everyone. Even psychologists can have emotional issues, in the same way that GPs aren't immune from catching a cold. If you have a physical pain and it keeps repeating or lasts for a long time, you might take a painkiller. If the pain doesn't go away, you go and talk to somebody about it. It's no different with emotional pain. When we don't make the time to stop and listen to ourselves, and to seek help when we need it, it's like compounding injury upon injury. Instead of repressing what we're experiencing, we need to learn to reframe our thinking so that we can heal. What's important is to recognise patterns of behaviour and understand how feelings can manifest physically as well as emotionally. This can help build resilience so that we are able to cope when the going gets tough.

We all have a fundamental need to feel seen, heard and validated by other people. It's necessary to develop relationships with others that fulfil these desires, but it's also important to make sure that we work just as hard on developing a similar level of connection with ourselves. The

Samaritans' principle of active listening was developed to soothe people in the moment; to ground them in a sense of safety and show them that, no matter what they say, they won't be judged; to let them know that what they are going through is valid, and that whatever they're thinking and feeling is acceptable and understandable. The aim of this journal is to help you apply these same aspects of empathy, compassion, validation and trust to yourself. If we practise these principles over time, we will keep ourselves on a more even keel.

Day to day, we listen to others to remind them that we care. We try and alleviate the worries of friends, family, loved ones and colleagues by giving them our full attention, or perhaps distracting them, and by keeping calm and using positive reinforcement. And yet, for some reason, our inner self-narrative is often unkind. The way we talk to ourselves can be completely at odds with the way we speak to others. In all the relationships that we develop throughout our lives, often the relationship with the self is the one that is most critical, particularly when we experience difficult thoughts and feelings.

Perhaps it's to do with the social conditioning that often comes in part from a well-meaning place. Picture a parent or teacher saying to a child, 'Don't cry' or 'Don't be so angry'. They say it because they don't want to see that little person in distress: it's upsetting, and they'd prefer to see the child feeling something more harmonious or positive. But what that teaches us, over time, is that we *shouldn't* be feeling those negative emotions, and so we learn to repress them. Going through tricky life experiences without an outlet can lead to an imbalance in our emotional wellbeing. This book will look at ways in which you can reconnect with yourself and explore some of those thoughts and feelings in a safe way.

Self-exploration

At Samaritans, we don't give advice. We try to help people recognise that we're all human, and we're all fallible. Instead of setting ourselves impossibly high standards, we should give ourselves a break from time to time and realise that, actually, what we're feeling is perfectly acceptable and probably a very valid response to whatever it is we're going through in our lives at this particular moment.

When we listen to people, we provide a haven in which they can work out what is going on for them and what they might like to do about it. Let's do the same here – the blank pages of this journal offer a neutral space in which you can explore whatever it is you want to, free from judgement. We might make a suggestion or two to encourage you along and help you to elaborate or clarify, but this is your journal, and this is your journey.

Hopefully you will learn that there are reasons – emotional, physical and neurological – that explain why you react the way you do, and once you understand them, you can begin to work out for yourself what could make you feel better. Healing, mental health and emotional wellbeing are incredibly personal journeys – there is no right or wrong in any of them. So, you do you. Discover what works best for your personality, values, lifestyle, likes and interests – and if something stops working, try something else. Building the habits of self-kindness and self-compassion can be done in many ways, and you have the power to choose what works best for you.

You know yourself better than anyone else, and therefore you know what it will take to get you to the place you want to be. You are strong enough to work out your own path. The route may be long and winding, and at times we all have moments when it's hard to see the wood for the trees. But it begins with one single step. By clarifying your own journey and process, you might even come to realise that things won't necessarily always feel the way they do right now. The brain is a wonderful tool, and with the right help you can begin to rewire it and retrain your thinking in a way that is beneficial to your body and mind. And if you ever feel like it's too hard to do alone, there is always someone there to listen.

This journal

Journaling is a very mindful activity and can occupy your headspace in a healthy way, allowing you to focus on the present moment without the need to worry about things that have happened in the past or panic about what could happen in the future.

Let this book be a reminder to explore what's going on in your life and prioritise time to focus on yourself (that's not a luxury, by the way: think of it more as a necessity). There are simple explanations, ideas, prompts and thoughts from Samaritans volunteers and specialists to help you discover more about yourself. There are pages for self-reflection, curiosity and creative expression. These can help you gain clarity on what you might be feeling and why, so that you can work towards lessening the negative feelings if or when they happen again.

Consider it a safe place to write, draw, doodle and make lists or word clouds of anything you want to put on the page. Remember: this is about the process, not a final piece of work. There is no pressure for you to write neatly or spell correctly. It is simply about connection: firstly, connecting your pen to the paper; then, connecting your thoughts to your emotions. We will learn about the importance of connecting to the present moment: how emotions connect to behaviours, how mind connects to body, and how we can listen to ourselves in the same way we would listen to someone else who needed to be heard.

Whatever ends up on the page will be beautiful in its own way. And if you don't like it, you can rub it out and start again – only you will ever know.

Please note: It's important to be aware that the aim and intention of this journal is not to diagnose or label in any way, or to question specific mental illnesses or disorders. It is in no way an alternative to making contact with Samaritans. If you are struggling and need support, please see the list of resources on pages 203-8.

'Two roads diverged in wood, and I–
I took the one less travelled by'

– ROBERT FROST

Chapter 1
You are safe

This journal is all about you finding your own path through the unique and personal journey that you are on. As you work your way through it, it is possible that negative thoughts or difficult memories may arise.

If at any point you find it hard to process anything that this journal or the words and prompts unearth, you might like to try some self-soothing exercises that involve regulating your breathing or visualising a safe place.

If you already have an idea of what works best for you to self-soothe or encourage a sense of calm, make some notes about it below.

If this isn't something you have done before, over the next few pages you will find suggestions for:

- a simple breathing exercise

- a visualisation exercise

- a muscle relaxation exercise.

There is also a personal plan on pages 16-17 that will help you recognise when your thoughts or feelings are becoming too much and you might need a little help. You can fill this in during a moment of calm and refer back to it at any point.

Notes:

. . . .

. . . .

Breathing exercise

You might want to sit for this, or you might prefer to lie down – do whatever helps you feel most relaxed.

You might feel more comfortable with your eyes closed, or you might want to keep them open – again, it's entirely up to you.

If you are sitting, feel your feet connect to the floor and your back connect to the chair. If you are lying down, feel your whole body connect to the floor.

Breathe in.

Hold.

Release.

Repeat.

Some people like to gently breathe in for four counts, softly hold for four and then slowly breathe out for six counts. You can work up to this.

Breath in. In your mind, say: *I know I am breathing in.*

Breathe out. In your mind, say: *I know I am breathing out.*

Feel how inhalation connects with exhalation.

Feel your muscles soften and relax as you breathe out.

Feel your body and your mind connect.

Feel any tension melting away.

Keep breathing in and then out, slowly and gently, for as long as you need.

Visualisation

Try and think of a place that represents a safe space for you. Imagine it in your mind. Choose somewhere that makes you feel comfortable and calm and is full of positive associations.

You might like to begin by gently breathing in for four counts and out for six to focus yourself. When your breathing has settled into a nice, relaxed rhythm, picture your safe space in your mind's eye.

You can do this with your eyes open or closed, sitting or standing, and you can think about absolutely anywhere that makes you feel good: it might be a sunny beach, it might be your living room, it could be a forest, it could be your car.

Alternatively, your safe space might be in the here and now, looking all the way around you and acknowledging that you are currently in a place that feels good for you. It's about what works for you. The important thing is to conjure up an image of this place and, as you breathe calmly, to know that, at any point, you can come back here in your mind and feel steady and content.

Describe your safe space in words:

• What does it look like?

. . . .

• What colours can you see?

. . . .

• What can you smell?

. . . .

• What can you feel?

. . . .

What can you hear?

. . . .

What does the ground beneath your feet feel like?

. . . .

You can stay with this image for as long as you like. Then, when you're ready, roll your shoulders back and around in a small circle: once, twice, three times. You might want to squeeze your shoulders up to your ears and let them drop as you breathe out. If you feel comfortable doing so, you could even stretch your arms all the way up above your head, reaching upwards and outwards, breathing all the way out as you gently bring your arms back down. Repeat this as many times as you like until you feel steady and ready to continue.

Remember that you can always come back to this place, whenever you want to.

If you would like to, draw a picture of your safe space:

Muscle relaxation exercise

Progressive muscle relaxation involves tensing and releasing pairs of muscles in sequence. It can help if you imagine all the tension leaving your body as you release your muscles. Some people find this helps them feel calmer and more grounded. You can practise it for any length of time.

- Find somewhere to sit, with your feet planted flat on the ground, shoulder-width apart. If you prefer, you can lie down instead.

- Take a deep breath in through your nose. Hold it for a few seconds, then breathe out slowly through your mouth.

- Try to keep your attention focused on your body. Notice any physical sensations you're feeling. Keep breathing all the way in and out, slowly and steadily.

- If you notice your mind wandering, acknowledge this is happening, then gently bring your focus back to your body.

- Start with the muscles in your head. Tense your forehead muscles by raising your eyebrows and holding them there for up to ten seconds. Breathe in as you tense these muscles.

- Now release, imagining tension leaving your body as you breathe out.

- Rest for a few seconds before moving on to the next group of muscles, working your way down your body. Start with the other muscles in your face, before moving down to your neck and shoulders, then on to your arms, your chest, your stomach, your legs and your feet. With each group of muscles, try to think of the tension just melting away.

When you've finished, don't get up straight away. Stay where you are for a minute or so. Then get up nice and slowly.

You can practise this technique whenever you notice yourself becoming stressed, upset or anxious.

Your personal plan

Fill in this plan at a time when you feel calm and comfortable, and refer back to it any time you are feeling overwhelmed.

How I know I am starting to feel upset, overwhelmed or uncomfortable:
For example, my heart might race, I might feel sick.

. . . .

If my thoughts and emotions overwhelm me at any point, what do I need in this moment?
To wrap myself in a blanket, cry, distract myself, call someone.

. . . .

Ways to distract myself:
Have a shower, go outside for a walk, make a plan for my day, make a list of achievable tasks.

. . . .

I can say to myself...
This will pass.

. . . .

I can ask for help by...
Talking to someone.

. . . .

Things that give me hope:
Write down a few notes about things that give you hope. These could be things you love, something you're looking forward to, or anything else that you find uplifting.

....

I can call:
Friends/loved ones/family/colleague/neighbour/support worker.

Name..

Phone number..

Name..

Phone number..

Name..

Phone number..

Name..

Phone number..

I am aware of local support services:
My GP/groups/sponsor/carer/therapist/counsellor (for ideas, see 'Where to seek further support' on pages 203–08)

....

In crisis, I can call Samaritans on 116 123, or I can email them at jo@samaritans.org. I can call 999 and ask for an ambulance if I need to.

Chapter 2
Values and listening

An introduction to Samaritans values

At Samaritans, we have five core values.

The first and most important is **listening**, because exploring feelings alleviates distress and helps people to reach a better understanding of their situation and the options open to them.

The second is **confidentiality** – if people feel safe, they are more likely to be open about their feelings.

The third is that we are **non-judgemental**, because we want people to be able to talk to us about whatever they need to without fear of prejudice or rejection, and to feel supported in making their own decisions wherever possible.

The fourth is that we believe that people have the right to **find their own solution**, and that telling people what to do takes responsibility and power away from them.

Finally, we believe in the importance of **human contact**, because giving people time, undivided attention and empathy meets a fundamental emotional need and reduces distress and despair.

Your personal values

Have a think about what your own values might be. Highlight some in the list opposite or add some of your own in the space beneath:

My personal values are...

honesty
humour
listening to others
safety
peace
responsibility
communication
independence
spirituality
friends
wisdom
achievement
knowledge
success
inspiring confidence

stability
family
wealth
free time
respect
power
authentic connection with others
creativity
reason
morality
love
beauty
not judging others
relaxation

You might like to set an intention here, for example:
I will use these values to guide my choices

Intention:

. . . .

. . . .

. . . .

Notes:

. . . .

. . . .

. . . .

Samaritans behaviours

At Samaritans, we work with the behaviours of support, trust, aspiration and respect. Think about how you might be able to apply these to your daily life.

I support myself by

....

I support others by

....

I trust myself to

....

I trust others to

....

I aspire to

....

Others aspire to be like me because

....

I respect myself by

....

I respect others by

....

How to listen to yourself

At Samaritans, we seek to listen and to understand. We help people open up about how they might be feeling by questioning, reacting, summarising, reflecting, clarifying and encouraging: listening to them in a way that encourages authentic conversation.

This can work just as well for self-exploration as it can when speaking to others, and it can help us to access and process our emotions. We can all learn to better listen to our own internal dialogue so that we can become more aware of what's going on within ourselves.

Good listening is about being interested in and focused on the person you are listening to: curious about what things feel like for them, accepting of what they tell you, and supporting them to keep going. Being properly listened to encourages someone to look at the small details in their own words: their passing comment or flippant reply can often mask something more significant. Why don't we try to do the same for ourselves? While we might be aware of the big ideas that tend to hog all our brain space, let's learn to listen to and register the smaller details that might have been part of our mind clutter.

Listening is active rather than passive. It takes time, care and attention. Self-care is no different, and we need to get into the habit of prioritising it in order to build good routines of awareness and acceptance. Listen to your body, listen to your thoughts, listen to your feelings. What are they telling you? Remember to look after your own mind as a priority and know that it is always possible to move forwards and find your way through difficult situations.

SHUSH

Our 'SHUSH' tips are an easy way of remembering the main points of active listening – let's see if we can apply them to listening to ourselves in the same way we would when listening to someone else.

S – Show you care
H – Have patience
U – Use open questions
S – Say it back
H – Have courage

Show you care

Make time for yourself, in which you can focus your full, undivided attention on you and only you. Show yourself how much you care by prioritising yourself. Switch off from distractions. Life can be extremely busy, and in this age of constant digital connectivity, multitasking has become the norm. We love our phones, but it's important to set yours to one side once in a while. Try to really focus on learning something new about you. Become aware of what your body and mind are doing and what you might be thinking or feeling. The aim here is to identify and accept your own thoughts and emotions, then understand how to respond to them with empathy and without judgement.

HOW WILL YOU SHOW YOURSELF YOU CARE?
For example, giving myself time to journal/switching off my phone/taking a break and going outside.

. . . .

. . . .

. . . .

Have patience

It may take time and several attempts at putting pen to paper before you get anywhere. Keep trying to find new ways of exploring your thoughts in a way that is comfortable for you. Don't give yourself a hard time if you don't yet know how to do this – treat yourself with compassion and patience, and remind yourself that this is a safe space for you to note down whatever you want to, whenever you want to. There is no rush. It might take a while before you are able to articulate what you're feeling. Try and relax into the process and just see what happens. Treat yourself with the same care and kindness you would show others when asking what's going on with them. Get into the good habit of telling yourself that whatever you are experiencing in this moment is real and valid.

Use open questions

Develop a good practice each day of asking yourself 'How am I feeling?' and 'What am I thinking?' Opening up about a problem can be difficult. You might not realise something is affecting you as much as it is – you might gloss over it, or try to hide the issue. You might not even know what the heart of the problem is until you have explored it. So find ways of being curious. Avoid asking yourself questions that will elicit a 'yes' or 'no' answer, such as 'Are you feeling OK?' Instead, use open-ended questions, such as 'How are you feeling today?' Questions like this might open up new avenues rather than shutting down your thought process. Then try to elaborate – keep exploring. Keep thinking, 'What else can I say about that?'

HOW ARE YOU FEELING TODAY?

. . . .

. . . .

Now elaborate by asking these open questions:
When – 'When did I realise I felt this way?'

. . . .

Where – 'Where did that happen?' or 'Where do I go when I start to feel like this?'

. . . .

What – 'What else happened?' or 'What do I think is making me feel this way?'

. . . .

How – 'How did that feel?'

. . . .

Say it back

Write down your feelings. Get your thoughts out of your head by putting them on paper. Explore your feelings and create an impression of them. If it feels comfortable, read your words out loud to yourself (or someone else, if you'd like to). Often, hearing ourselves say something out loud can help us process our thoughts in a different way, because we hear it back differently. Reflect on what you've written or drawn (whether that's your answers to the prompts above, or anywhere else in this journal), to check you understand what you've created. Clarify it if you need to. Is there anything else you'd like to add? Would you like to try expressing yourself in a different way? Try to really acknowledge everything you see in what you've written or drawn. This can help you understand the circumstances that surround your emotional responses.

Have courage

Self-exploration might feel a little daunting. But rather than repressing an issue, have the confidence to open up. Think of these pages as a safe, neutral space where you can say whatever it is you want to without fear of judgement. And if you need some help to explore difficult issues that arise in a more structured way with someone else, check back to your personal plan on page 16-17. Remember not to be too harsh on yourself – sometimes, we are our own toughest critics! Give yourself a break from the pressure and strains of day-to-day life and prioritise a moment, no matter how small or how generous, in which to express yourself in whatever way you feel comfortable. Get into the habit of positive self-talk, reminding yourself that you *can* do this, you *can* connect with yourself, you *can* express how you're feeling, and that self-care *is* a priority. Remind yourself that whatever comes up, it's OK to feel the way you do, and you can take your time or step away if it ever feels too tricky.

'Mighty oaks from little acorns grow'

– ANONYMOUS

Your goals

Think about what you would like to achieve from using this journal, and consider the small steps you can take towards this goal. You can either choose from some suggestions below, or write your own. Just writing down your intentions can be the first milestone. There is space at the back of the book to create more lists if you'd like to.

I will use this book to:
• develop a more positive mindset

• remember to be kind to myself as well as others

• understand more about how my brain and emotions are connected

• practise good habits, such as self-care and kindness

• keep track of my moods

• feel more hopeful

• connect better with myself

• learn more about my own emotional wellbeing

• develop good habits of self-compassion and empathy.

. . . .

. . . .

. . . .

. . . .

• What is it that you truly want?

. . . .

. . . .

. . . .

• Do you think you are capable of achieving it?

. . . .

. . . .

. . . .

• What advice would you give to someone else in the same position?

. . . .

. . . .

. . . .

• What are some small steps you might be able to take towards a bigger goal?

. . . .

. . . .

. . . .

Chapter 3
Wellbeing and balance

The emotional health scale

There are many formal psychological ways of describing how emotionally 'well' we are. At Samaritans, we use a less official emotional health scale that looks a bit like doorstop wedge. It's a really useful way of understanding how every single person, every single day, at any given time, is in an ongoing state of emotional health, of which there are many moving parts: different life events, personal issues, relationships, work, health, etc. These things may be external or internal. There may be things over which we have some measure of control, and others over which we have no control at all. They all impact on and influence us. Sometimes this impact is positive, but if we experience a negative event, it can have a significant effect on our ability to cope. The impact it has can vary depending on where we are that day on the emotional health scale.

We all slide up and down this scale – it's a constantly moving dynamic. We might go up and down within an hour, or within a day, or over short periods of time. Problems can begin when a lot of events and circumstances push us further and further down the scale. When a number of issues snowball, we become weakened, distressed and destabilised. As a result, we will have a number of physical and emotional reactions, which could make it very difficult to climb back up the scale by ourselves. This can manifest within us in different ways, from internalising what's going on and feeling a sense of numbness or withdrawal, to experiencing stress and anxiety. Over time, this can erode our self-esteem, confidence, sense of self and sense of worth, so that we no longer feel capable, worthy or equipped to cope.

What's really important to understand is that we all experience things differently. Someone else might be able to cope very easily with what's going on, and may not necessarily understand why you are where you are on the scale, or why something is a big deal for you, or why you feel the way you do. There is a simple reason for this – it's because they're not you. They're not living your life; they're not walking in your footsteps. They're not dealing with whatever your personal set of circumstances might be, and these are the factors that influence whether you feel like you can cope with the extra pressure of, say, a broken washing machine.

For some people, in the grand scheme of things, having to deal with a broken washing machine might be an annoying addition to their to-do list, but it's not a catastrophe. It *is* catastrophic, though, if you're at the lower end of the emotional health scale, or you've got no money, or are trying to wash some clothes for a job interview, or if you're feeling distressed about how well you're parenting your children if you can't give them clean clothes.

Wherever you are on the scale bears no relation to where anybody else might be. What matters is recognising where you are, and understanding what you can do about it. We can give ourselves a head start on our ability to stay within the middle to top realms of the scale by making sure we're keeping a good balance of the internal and external factors that might affect us. To do this, we can check in with ourselves every day, or even several times a day, to see where we are on the emotional health scale. We need to give ourselves permission to take the time to ask: what's going on for me at the moment? What are the different things I am having to deal with? Can I cope with these things alone, or do I need to ask for support?

If you like, you can use the scale as an anchor tool throughout this book, coming back to it to check in and see where you are on the scale as you go along. You might notice that there are some moments when your resilience is much higher, when you're at the top end of the scale. If that happens, perhaps you could think about what you're like when you are at your best – what the best *you* looks like, which external and internal circumstances are most helpful to *you* when it comes to feeling balanced. Sometimes trying to make your way back up the scale might feel like trying to climb a mountain. So, let's plan some strategies in the calmer moments to help you climb back up to the top when you find yourself slipping down the scale.

Strength

Struggling to cope   Coping very well

At the top end of the scale, where you feel good and able to deal with whatever is going on day to day, you might notice you are using language like 'I will' or 'I can'. At the lower end of the scale, you might start to use words like 'I'll try to' or 'I can't' or 'I tried that before, I don't know if I can'. Over time, it's possible to learn to recognise if and when you begin to doubt yourself, so keep being curious and stay aware of how you're feeling day to day.

The wellbeing scale

How would you rate your level of emotional wellbeing on a scale between 1 (I'm fine) and 10 (I'm feeling awful)?

Fine   1   2   3   4   5   6   7   8   9   10   Awful

Emotional wellbeing can mean different things for different people. Some might be aware that they are experiencing sadness, stress, anxiety or worry and will recognise what leads to an increase in particular patterns of moods or behaviours. Others might be at the beginning of the journey of recognising, or wanting to recognise, these ups and downs and what they might mean. Have a think about how well you know your emotional states and use the scale below to try and measure where you are between feeling 'fine' at one end and 'awful' at the other. If you're at a 3, you might recognise you're feeling a bit down, but it will likely pass. But if you're at a 7 or 8 perhaps things are really getting on top of you and you might want to reach out to a trusted person for support or to talk things through. If you're at 10 and feeling really bad, know that it's OK to be honest about the depth of your feelings and ask for help – refer back to your personal plan and remember that there is always someone there to listen.

Use this space to write down why you think you might be feeling this way, or if there's anything else you would like to explore.

. . . .

. . . .

. . . .

I am thinking...

. . . .

. . . .

. . . .

I am feeling...

. . . .

. . . .

. . . .

You can come back to this scale and check in whenever you like – perhaps you could make it a regular practice?

Balance

' Mental health doesn't discriminate: it can affect anyone. It is important that we do what we can: acknowledging the difficulty of how things are, practising self-compassion, cultivating meaningful relationships, and taking the lead in our own wellbeing journeys. I work with people who have mild to moderate mental-health difficulties, such as depression, panic, phobias, insomnia and stress. Emotional resilience and emotional intelligence are essential tools that need to be cultivated by building awareness of self and developing helpful coping skills in order to take care of yourself in the best way you can. While there is appropriate care out there, it might not be accessible for everyone, so it's important to take the lead in your journey, or in your recovery.

During the Covid pandemic, people had a lot of time to sit with uncomfortable emotions. These could be a wide range of things that might have been bubbling beneath the surface for some time, but had been buried by the noise of work or travel or community activities. These things coming to the surface has been scary for a lot of people. It forced a lot of self-reflection.

We need to be more in tune with ourselves and really work on finding a balance, however that looks for each of us as individuals. Perhaps you have reflected on what's really important to you over the various lockdowns and can see that your priorities have shifted. It's good to question where you want to put your energy and time, and to consider what's meaningful to you.

Life does not always have to be an equal balance. Depending on what season of life we're in, some things may take more precedence and others may go on the back burner. However, we need to have a balance between things like work and the other responsibilities that define us, and the things we enjoy, because when our mental health deteriorates, hobbies or creative pursuits are one of the first things to go. This is often because we feel guilty about taking time for ourselves, or simply lack the energy.

So, take the time to check in and reflect on whether your life feels balanced. Sometimes this can be as simple as asking yourself: are my physical needs met? Am I hungry? Am I well-rested? In addition, you can ask: do I feel overwhelmed by my job/parenting/studies? What do I need to practise doing less or more of?

If we don't have balance, we are not able to cope when the stress and pressures of life increase. This can cause us to engage in unhelpful behaviours, which just exacerbate our difficulties. Imagine you are sailing a boat. When the sea gets choppy, holes appear in your boat, causing it to take on water. To stop the boat from sinking, you try to bail out the water. But you're so focused on bailing that you stop being aware of the direction in which you are sailing. Suddenly, you realise you're really far off course. Then you might notice that the bucket you are using to bail out the water is itself full of holes: what you are using to try and solve your problem is just maintaining it! Perhaps there are other tools you need, as the one you've been trying to use hasn't worked. To keep your boat afloat, you need to identify the right tools to maintain balance, so that even when you do take water on, the boat won't sink.

– Jessica, Bexley and Dartford branch
  and psychological wellbeing practitioner

What is weighing you down?
For example, work, relationships, debt, illness.

. . . .

. . . .

How can you balance out the heavy weights?
*For example, relaxation, support networks, hobbies, creativity, speaking
to someone.*

. . . .

. . . .

What would you like more of in your life?

. . . .

. . . .

What do you need to let go of?

. . . .

. . . .

What brings you joy?

. . . .

. . . .

THE WHEEL OF LIFE
Draw a circle and divide it up like a pie.

Label the pieces with all the different aspects of your life, for example work, family, leisure, health and creativity.

Reflect on what you've drawn and ask yourself: Where am I out of balance? Where am I willing to give? Where can I take some time to move into a different segment?

Self check-in:
How are you feeling physically?

Do you ever experience any of the following physical sensations, feelings or symptoms? Perhaps you could highlight the ones you feel *often* in one colour, and the ones you feel *sometimes* in another colour:

- aching muscles
- back pain
- churning stomach
- digestive issues
- faster breathing
- feeling really tired
- feeling sick
- grinding your teeth
- headache
- pins and needles
- racing heartbeat
- restlessness
- stress
- sweating
- trouble sleeping.

Use this space to write down any other physical sensations in your body.

. . . .

. . . .

. . . .

. . . .

. . . .

Self check-in:
How are you feeling emotionally?

Use this space to write down or draw any emotions you are feeling at this moment. This can include:
• thoughts
• images
• changes in your mood
• changes in habits or behaviours (*for example, sleeping poorly, feeling exhausted, being tearful or arguing more with people*)
• anything at all.

....

....

....

....

....

....

Communicating without words

‘Creativity is about how we take in the world. It is an essential part of being human. We are constantly using our imaginations, and it's important to be able to use them in a way that doesn't feel burdensome, but rather in a way that liberates us. If we encourage creativity to flow, it opens us up to possibility and trust, and that can be really empowering.

Doodling, colouring in or simply making marks with a pen on the page can provide a very safe, contained way of exploring our feelings. Imagine the arts as a container for feelings that may be beyond words: those things that are hard to make sense of, or that you feel other people might not understand. Or perhaps there's something that's overwhelming you, but you're just not ready to share with anyone else. An image, doodle or symbol is a way of putting something out there so that it's not just inside you. The paper can hold some part of what you're trying to make sense of. Over time, you may be able to understand it; you may even be able to find words for it. What's important is the process of expressing something that's going on inside.

However you choose to put something on paper, there is no right or wrong. It's not about being an artist: it's about the process. What's important is noticing how you feel as you create. Notice how the pen feels in your hand, and how you feel as you look at what you are putting down on paper. Just keep going with it, and notice what happens.

Art is a safe way of making sense of what you're feeling. A lot of my work is about creating a safe space, just as Samaritans do. People can then start to find their voice and discover ways of helping themselves. At the beginning, it can feel messy. When I work with someone, I'll often say, ‘Do we need to make something safe to hold the mess?’ Then people can create an actual container to put all their work in. This gives them a boundary, and that helps everything feel a bit more manageable.

You could apply the same principle here – draw a shape to hold your feelings. This is your safe space. Inside the shape, draw, doodle or simply make marks with a pen. There's no need to feel self-conscious about the art: just think about connecting with whatever it is you want to put into your safe place. It's somewhere you can put things so that they don't have to go back into you. Whatever you say, it won't hurt the paper – so you can say whatever you want.

Take time to reflect on what you see. Don't judge it as a piece of art, but think about what it says about you. Do these little sketches or tiny shapes represent something significant about you and your life, such as how little space you take up? Whatever you create is like a mirror. Sometimes creating can give you a sense of distance, and you might use an image or a character to express something you're not quite ready to open up to directly. That sense of being one step removed can really help you access a different perspective.

People are complicated. We have so much we're experiencing and feeling, and we often don't have the language to express it. The arts offer a way for us to express ourselves without having to worry about getting the words 'right' or understandable. Often the people I work with leave feeling like they've managed to release something, and that can feel like a weight has been lifted off their shoulders.

– Anthea Benjamin, UKCP art therapist

DRAW YOURSELF A CONTAINER

Make a shape – a square, a circle, anything you like – to ring-fence your safe space. Then put whatever you want inside: a pattern, colours, dots, dashes, a picture. You don't have to think of it as art – it's simply an exercise for you to see how it feels to put pen or pencil to the paper.

SQUIGGLES

Begin by drawing a line. Keep the line going. All the way up and across the page. Curl the line, turn it back on itself, fold it in and out of the other lines, circle it around, swoop and arc all over the page, in any direction you like, until the paper is full of squiggles. The squiggles can be as big or as small as you want – there is no right or wrong way of doing this.

When the page is full of squiggles, have a look and see if you can see any shapes or pictures within the lines. Think of it like the game of spotting shapes in the clouds. Draw around any images you see, or simply colour in the shapes the squiggles have made.

How did you feel when you were drawing the squiggles?

. . . .

. . . .

. . . .

How did you feel when you were colouring in the shapes or pictures?

. . . .

. . . .

. . . .

Chapter 4
Emotions and self-empathy

Naming your feelings

Putting a name to what you are feeling can often help you understand what you might be thinking. Have a look at the words and phrases below, and circle or star the ones you recognise or identify with. Perhaps you could highlight the ones you feel *often* in one colour, and the ones you feel *sometimes* in another colour.

afraid	left out
amused	like I don't fit in
angry	like I'm a burden
anxious	lonely
apathetic	lost
bored	neutral
content	on edge
defeated	overwhelmed
disappointed	panicked
disconnected	peaceful
down	regretful
energised	satisfied
frustrated	stressed
happy	stuck
hopeful	tense
hopeless	thankful
humiliated	trapped
joyful	I don't know

Emotions

Did you know there are six basic emotions?
happiness
sadness
fear
disgust
anger
surprise

What colour do you think these emotions are?
Is anger always red? Is sadness always blue? Write the name of an emotion in one of the circles below, then colour in or pattern it with the colours that best represent the emotion for you:

Of course, there are a whole range of other things we feel too, such as: *optimistic, defensive, apprehensive, loving, enraged, joyful, terrified, trusting, remorseful, critical, annoyed, impatient, aggressive, peaceful, hopeful, accepting, disapproving, bored.*

Think of some other things that you might feel and jot them down here:

. . . .

. . . .

. . . .

Now pick one or two of the feelings that stand out to you and write a few lines about your understanding of what each one means: how it might make you feel physically, how it might affect your thoughts.

. . . .

. . . .

. . . .

You might like to try a word game to explore further, such as an acrostic poem, where you use each letter of the word to start a sentence, or a new word. For example, here's an acrostic poem for the word 'hope':

H – how to have
O – optimism and
P – positivity
E – every day.

Would you like to give it a go? Use the space below.

Understanding our emotions

Our emotional state is constantly fluctuating. Sometimes, our sadness might be caused by something tangible, like shock or grief. At other times, we might be cross due to pure exhaustion, or find ourselves crying tears of anger. Our level of surprise will differ depending on what prompts the reaction, and our fear will probably correspond to the size of the perceived threat.

You might like to try this exercise to help you understand what different emotions mean to you, and how they might appear. For example:

What is the point of sadness?
It tells me when I need to feel loved and valued.

Sadness can show up as:
Feeling tired, a sense of being alone or feeling lonely, unhappiness, being restless or bored, feeling ignored.

What is the point of anger?
It shows that I am responding strongly to what I think is a negative situation.

Anger can look like:
Frustration, shouting, becoming withdrawn.

What is the point of fear?
It protects us from danger.

Fear can look like:
Worrying, insecurity, being scared, feeling anxiety and unease.

Now you give it a go:

. . . .

. . . .

What emotions can feel like in the body

Your body and mind are connected. Over the next few pages, we can begin to learn a little more about the kind of signals your mind sends to your body that correspond with your feelings. But first, have a think about how you feel physically when you experience different emotions, and compare that to the way you might feel emotionally. You can describe your feelings however you like, with just a word, or a sentence, and you might like to pick some words from the word clouds on the next page if that's helpful.

EMOTION	THOUGHTS	BEHAVIOURS
Anger		
Sadness		
Happiness		
Surprise		
Disgust		
Fear		

You might like to choose from these word clouds:

Physical

Faint, flushed, achey, heart racing, tearful, headache, back pain, sensitive, unsteady, open, tense, still, exhausted, sweaty palms, tense neck, soft, relaxed, tender, alert, muscle pain, fidgety, trembling, energetic, jumpy, steady, cold, hot, need to move, tight jaw, shivering, lump in throat, chest pain, guts churning, weak, sick, tired, heavy, can't sleep, shaky, restless, urge to bite fingernails.

Emotional

Irritated, scared, sad, guilty, courageous, unable to focus, satisfied, excited, lonely, unwanted, proud, inferior, distant, angry, in awe, apathetic, insecure, curious, abandoned, peaceful, anxious, disapproving, optimistic, confused, shocked, despairing, joyful, critical, awful, depressed, unmotivated, sensitive.

Feel your feelings – don't think them

Your emotions are a reaction, not a choice. It's important to acknowledge and accept them in the moment. Try this exercise to look at how you might express rising feelings, thoughts or emotions, and how you might validate them as being real and necessary to process. The first few have been filled in as an example.

If I feel... *sad*
I will... *cry*

If I feel... *anxious*
I will... *recognise it and try to breathe calmly*

If I feel... *lonely*
I will... *try to connect with someone and talk*

If I feel
I will. . . . .

If I feel
I will. . . . .

If I feel
I will. . . . .

If I feel
I will. . . . .

Self-empathy and the ladder of hope

As Samaritans, we try to get alongside the people we are listening to. Our aim isn't to save anybody, but rather to stand alongside them until they're ready to save themselves. It can help to imagine someone who's having a hard time – perhaps feeling low, stressed, depressed or anxious – as if they're sitting in a pit. What friends and family might do, with the best of intentions, is try and pull them out of the pit. Our instinct is to run and get a ladder, put it into the pit and say, 'Hey, come on up here! It's much better where I am. Let me drag you up and out of the dark hole you're in.' Of course, the person suffering knows that it's all blue skies and green grass where you are; they know it's nice up there. But that makes them feel worse, because if they had any means of getting out of the pit, they would have surely done it by now.

A Samaritan would still run and get the ladder, but rather than saying, 'Come on, mate, put your foot on the first rung and take my hand, let's get you out,' they would climb down the ladder, into the pit and sit alongside the person, to simply say, 'I'm here.' They would then explore with the person what the pit feels like, using open questions, such as, 'What does it look like for you?'. If the reply is 'Dark', they would get the person to elaborate, perhaps by saying, 'What does "dark" mean to you?' The person might then say, 'Dark and scary.' And they can explore further, together, discovering how that looks and feels, and how it might be affecting them. When the person has explored all the avenues of thoughts and feelings they want to, they will naturally form a conclusion about what it is they want to do next. They might say, 'Perhaps I'm ready now to sit on the first step of the ladder.' And that small step can often lead to a big change.

It's possible to apply this idea to ourselves too. Self-empathy is also about getting alongside yourself, rather than looking at yourself from the perspective of how you think other people will be looking at you.

It's seeing yourself where you *are*, rather than where you think you *should be*. It's understanding that you might be different from the past you and the future you. Accept who you are *now*, and let go of the fear of judgement or differing views of others. Just focus on yourself.

Imagine for a moment that the person looking down into the pit is you, and that getting down into the pit is allowing yourself to feel whatever it is you want to feel in that moment. Don't judge yourself for how you're feeling. Don't try to hide from your thoughts. Let them lead you, but question yourself. Ask: 'What does this look like to me? What does this feel like for me? What could that mean? What is it that has made me feel this way? What else do I have to say about it?'

Then, thinking about the tools available to you, write a word on each rung of the ladder that might help you gently begin to get up and out of the pit. They can be absolutely anything: verbs of what you might do, such as singing, cooking or working; adjectives, like strength and hope; or nouns, like rest, hydration, medication, counsellor or GP.

Elaborate

We can use the technique of open questions we explored in the Ladder of Hope exercise on page 49 to explore our feelings and help us understand them better. Think of a particular issue or emotion, then fill in the blanks below to see if you can explore and elaborate on your thoughts.

When I am (*write an emotion here*) . . . .

It makes me feel . . . .

. . . .

Say a little more about what it feels like. When you say it's . . . . ,
what does that mean?

. . . .

. . . .

. . . .

Can you elaborate on that any further?

. . . .

. . . .

. . . .

It makes me think . . . .

. . . .

Say a little more about those thoughts. When you say it makes you think
. . . . , what does that mean?

. . . .

. . . .

. . . .

Can you elaborate on that any further?

. . . .

. . . .

. . . .

It looks like . . . .

Say a little more about how it looks. When you say it looks . . . . ,
what does that mean?

. . . .

. . . .

. . . .

Can you elaborate on that any further?

. . . .

. . . .

. . . .

Emotional intelligence

' I've been a Samaritans listening volunteer for about eight years now. In my day job, I'm a business and occupational psychologist. One thing I've found, both as a coach and as a Samaritan, is that it's useful for people to recognise that mental wellbeing is a continuum. Our emotional state and our ability to cope – or not – is constantly shifting, whether we're at work, dealing with a complex issue, or just handling the everyday. It can seem quite sudden when people realise that they are distressed, not just stressed. They may feel less able to see what their future or their true identity is, and it can be hard for them to understand what led them to that point.

Self-reflection, whether through journaling or talking, is often the first step to being able to help ourselves by increasing our self-awareness. This kind of reflection deserves time and practice, and it's really important that we make that time for ourselves. Whether you flood the pages with words or images, record a stream of consciousness in ungrammatical sentences, or write down single words, all of these things can gradually calm the noise inside your mind. Getting into the habit of documenting your feelings legitimises the need to set aside a little time and space to better connect to yourself.

As you journal, consider this your journey. Imagine you are getting on a train at a station, and no one can contact you while you're travelling from point A to point B. The transition between there and here is yours and yours alone – visualise yourself leaving the station, secure in the knowledge that you'll get off at the right stop, and, in the meantime, you can do anything and be anyone you like. You get to define the bit in the middle.

You could try thinking of one particular issue you'd like to deal with and ask yourself what your priorities are within that – what you find difficult, whether you are where you want to be, and if you'd like to make a change. You can then use these ideas as starting points for further conversations with other people, or the beginning of a conversation with yourself.

Being aware of your emotions is so important, because if you know 'I'm worried about this' or 'I've got that on my mind', you can understand that maybe now isn't the best time to be doing something complicated that needs care and attention, because your feelings are colouring your view. For example, if my child is being cheeky, I might ordinarily laugh and tell them to stop being cheeky, but if I've got this other thing going on in my head, I might snap at them. Having self-awareness can help us interpret the cues and the interactions around us, and then choose more consciously how we would like to respond. If we can be aware of how we're feeling, at the very least we can cut ourselves a bit of slack, or be more honest with those around us and tell them we're struggling. They may be more willing and able to help than we might have thought.

It's more than OK to say, 'You know what, I'm feeling bad. I'm going to just crash under the duvet and say "Go away, world", switch my phone off and see how I feel in the morning.' But if I haven't even clocked that that's how I'm feeling, I might just keep forging on, being cross and angry and feeling bad. Over time, self-awareness will help us to adapt and shift our behaviour in a way that is more kind to ourselves, and to other people too.

– **Karen, Guildford branch, business/occupational psychologist**

If you're feeling terrible, tell yourself about it. Say it out loud. Write it down. Explore it. Accept it. Acknowledge that you know yourself far better than anyone else knows you, and therefore you are the best person to make the right decisions about what to do next. Remind yourself that you might need help or guidance, but ultimately, you have the power to get out of the pit.

If you find this exercise too overwhelming or difficult to do, remember your personal plan on pages 16-17. Know that you have someone to turn to, and there is always someone to listen.

WHAT ARE YOU MOST AFRAID OF?

....

....

....

....

....

WHAT WOULD YOU DO IF YOU WERE REALLY BRAVE?

....

....

....

....

....

TAKE ONE PARTICULAR ISSUE YOU'D LIKE TO DEAL WITH AND ASK YOURSELF:

What are my priorities at the moment?

....

....

What am I finding most difficult?

....

....

What are some of the options available to me?

....

....

Am I where I want to be?

....

....

What one step would help me move in a more positive direction?

....

....

Chapter 5
The brain and the body.

The problem with neurobiology

The brain is an amazing tool, and scientists are learning more and more about it each and every day. We know much more now than we used to, and current neurobiology developments are blowing old theories out of the water. In an interview for this book, I heard the brain described as being 'on a level computer science can't even dream about'. So, clearly, we're not quite there yet with knowing everything we need to in scientific terms… But the idea here is to provide enough context to reassure you (without sending you to sleep or making you want to hurl this book into the nearest bin) that your physiological response is normal.

We're going to miss out a whole bunch of important bits, because, like I said, this isn't a biology class. So, let's skip straight to the good parts to try and demonstrate why the brain reacts rationally, and sometimes irrationally, to our emotional state. We'll be focusing on the following key areas:

• The reptilian brain (survival of the species instincts)
• The limbic/mammalian brain (emotional/behavioural response)
• The amygdala (fire-alarm system)
• The prefrontal cortex (reasoning, personality and decision making)
• Brain stem (controls breath and heartbeat)

You will hear these terms throughout the book, so we will explore them further over the next few pages. If you like, you can choose areas that interest you to read more about another time. Or you can choose to skip this section – it's totally up to you.

When people talk about the 'reptilian' brain, they are referring to the most primal bit of our brain. Think of it as the base, central part that deals with automatic, instinctive impulse and response. It taps into

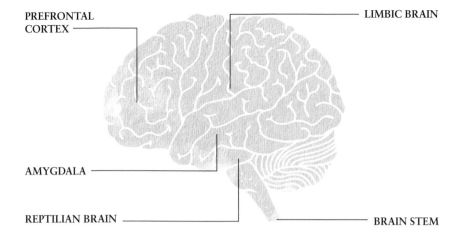

PREFRONTAL CORTEX

LIMBIC BRAIN

AMYGDALA

REPTILIAN BRAIN

BRAIN STEM

the idea of 'survival of the species' and controls our innate instinct for self-preservation, as well as our basic drives – things like feeding, fleeing, fighting... and reproduction. The brainstem, which controls our heartbeat, breathing and facial expressions, is part of the reptilian area.

The bit in the middle is referred to as the 'limbic' or 'mammalian' brain. This part basically deals with emotional and behavioural response and memory. This is where you'll find the amygdala, which plays a role in processing emotions, and the hippocampus, which stores memories. The limbic system helps the body respond to our emotions through instinctive behaviours such as 'fight or flight', caring for the young and connecting with others.

The 'neocortex' is the wrinkly bit on the top of the brain – people talk about this layer as the rational part that deals with speech and conscious thought, such as reasoning and analysis. As part of this, the 'prefrontal cortex' at the front of your brain looks after self-control, decision-making, planning and problem-solving.

Obviously, we don't have three separate brains – the parts described above all work together. But while for neuroscientists these groupings might not be perfect, and a new development discovered tomorrow could completely redefine the terms, hopefully what you can glean from these simple descriptions is that different parts of the brain, in general, do different things that correspond with our emotional state.

The fear factor

The emotional response in our bodies is actually quite a primitive, biological thing. Our inbuilt response mechanism can have a very real effect on us, physically as well as in our minds.

Emotional response begins in the amygdala – a small, almond-shaped region in the middle of your brain. In the face of a perceived threat, the amygdala fires up a response that triggers your nervous system. Think of it as a smoke alarm with a sprinkler system. Basically, you get flooded with adrenaline, which is helpful for the primal survival instinct we developed as cave people, as it makes you stronger and faster and helps you escape.

The physical sensation that accompanies this rush of hormones is an increase in blood pressure. Your heart begins to beat faster to get oxygen and sugar to your muscles, sweating increases as the blood flow changes, and your lungs work harder as you breathe. Your stomach and guts might churn, blood vessels dilate and muscles tense. You may shake, turn pale or flushed, and/or get a dry mouth.

This response, known as 'fight or flight' was a necessary function for our ancestors, who needed that extra boost of strength when hunting or fleeing from a predator. In some situations today, it is still necessary for us to use strength in the face of challenge or adversity: athletes about to run a race, or firefighters as they enter a burning building, for example. But what if you're not a gladiator? Or a boxer? Or rescuing someone who's fallen in a river? This same stress response can occur in reaction to just the thought of something scary – and when it does, our bodies react to it in the same way.

In the short term, the stress response can be helpful. When we're facing a crisis, it can help us power through: it can be what enables us to get up each day, put one foot in front of the other, and do all the things we need to do. This is unfeasible for the long term, though, and when the adrenaline from a fight-or-flight situation dissipates, we are suddenly exhausted, and our energy crashes.

Most of the time, we are able to self-regulate. But sometimes, a stress-response episode can reoccur. Like a fuse that keeps tripping the wrong way, the response can become harder to switch off, and can result in anxiety, fear, depression or aggression. Our perception can become skewed – we might feel like we're totally out of control, or we might battle for extreme control to try and alter the situation. Repeat episodes of these kinds of feelings – the combination of emotional reaction and physical response – are known as panic attacks.

Externalising helps us to label emotions, articulate them and, in doing so, process thoughts from the feeling part of the brain (limbic) to the thinking part (prefrontal cortex). Once the thinking part of the brain is back in action, we start to find solutions, because we're not so overwhelmed.

So, as you can see, fear is a very normal response, but when the fuse has tripped, we can get stuck in a cycle of being afraid of the physical reaction, which then perpetuates the fear feelings. Our resistance to facing fears is often what magnifies them. What we can try and work towards is acknowledging and accepting the cycle when it's happening. We can try to gently remind ourselves that it won't last forever, and do things like breathing exercises (see exercise below) or taking small sips of water to pull us back to the present moment. We can treat ourselves kindly and with compassion, and try to remind our minds that here and now, we are safe, in this moment, with our feet planted firmly on the ground.

There are different ways of processing fear that will be unique to us as individuals – sometimes we can burn it off through movement, sometimes we can learn to ride the wave of anxiety and understand that it will pass. Sometimes Cognitive Behavioural Therapy (CBT) can help, and sometimes a GP or therapist can help advise on how to manage if the feelings persist.

Breathing exercise: Calming breath

Breathing six times a minute (breathing in for five seconds and out for five seconds each time) has been shown to improve the heart's ability to respond better to stress and calm down once the immediate 'threat' has passed.

If you would like to, you can try this breathing practice:

Three times a day, take six breaths a minute for five minutes. You can do this exercise if you're feeling overwhelmed by the fight-or-flight response or any other kind of anxiety or worry. Have a look at page 137 for some other breathing exercises.

The nervous system

Another part of our physical make-up that can be helpful to understand is the nervous system. It's made up of two parts – the parasympathetic nervous system and the sympathetic nervous system.

First of all, let's try this exercise:

Remember a time when you experienced a particular emotion, like stress, anger or sadness. Just choose one for now – you can always come back and do the exercise again, thinking about a different emotion. Try to recall how this emotion felt in certain areas of your body, and make some notes, for example: *pupils dilated, stomach churned, breath quickened, heart beat faster.*

Emotion:. . . . .

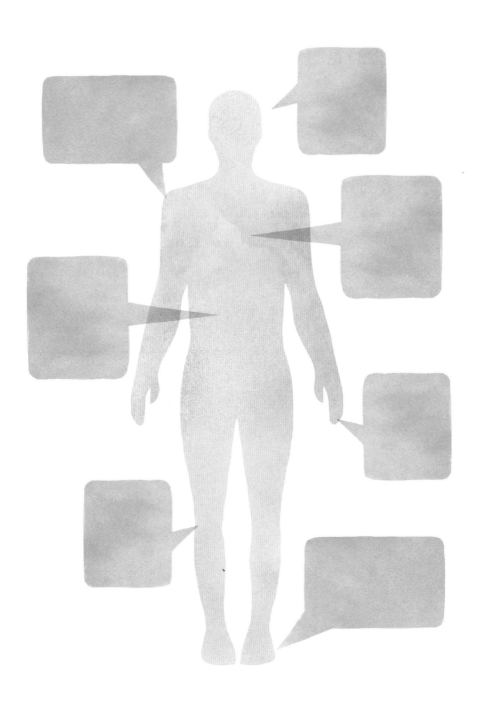

Now, let's look at *why* we might have the kinds of reactions you just described. It can be helpful to think of the sympathetic nervous system as the part that *creates* a physical stress reaction, and the parasympathetic nervous system as the calming part. They basically both control the same internal organs, but to completely different effect. Where the sympathetic nervous system is connected to the spine, the parasympathetic nervous system is connected directly to the brain. Within the parasympathetic nervous system, there is a nerve called the vagus nerve (pronounced like Las Vegas), which is a very long nerve that runs throughout the body and affects or activates our states of stress. There is a lot of helpful information out there if you want to look into these terms in more detail, but what's important to know is that we want to keep the two main parts of the nervous system in balance so that we aren't continually experiencing a fear and stress reaction, but can instead rest and find a place of tranquillity.

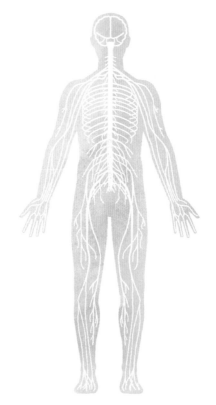

'Our life is shaped by our mind;
we become what we think'

– BUDDHA

The link between the body and the brain

' Stress is the body preparing to take action. If our brains perceive threat, we instantly release massive electro-chemical bodily solutions that enable us to fight or flee, and therefore survive. As listening volunteers at Samaritans, we often hear from people who have acquired stress habits due to their life's circumstances, but haven't yet learned how to manage them.

Habitual stress can become distressing. One thing we can say is, 'It's OK, it's understandable to have that response or even feel out of control. It will pass. Let it pass.'

Being told that your feelings are valid immediately reduces levels of cortisol (the stress hormone), brings your blood pressure down and reduces your overall stress response. If you imagine seeing someone in a stressed state, you can track the symptoms as they cascade through the body – the shoulders go up, the person hunches forward, their pupils dilate. Tension can make itself known in the form of tummy aches, bladder or bowel problems and other aches and pains. Fists and jaws clench, and movement is either super-fast or super-slow.

It's important to realise that all brains favour thoughts, feelings and behaviours that have become familiar to us, because to the primitive (reptilian) brain, familiar things can be predicted. Often, the physical responses described above become chronic because a person has habitually prepared their reptilian brain for fight or flight, but without any fight or flight action actually following. This means the body holds on to this powerful stress chemistry instead of getting rid of it. Continuous states of tension can become the new normal quite quickly, leading to mental, physical and emotional problems. Asking questions about the physical signals of stress may help bring respite to a Samaritans caller, and this is important because no one makes good decisions or thinks clearly when they are extremely stressed. We can help people reverse-engineer their physiology by enquiring about how they're breathing. For example, very stressed breathing is fast and shallow, so we can suggest they breathe slowly into the lower lobes of their lungs. Doing this sends a strong de-stress signal to the amygdala via the vagus nerve, which sits under the diaphragm. I try to explain it as clearing the cache – to just stop, take a breath, pause.

The part of the brain we really need to know about is the prefrontal cortex, which is where we start to become aware of ourselves consciously, whereas the reptilian and mammalian brain actions are largely unconscious. A metaphor for how our brains work is horse riding, where the rider represents the conscious mind (prefrontal cortex) and the horse represents the unconscious mind (reptilian and mammalian brain). The rider gives instructions and thinks they are in control. The horse is a huge, powerful creature, and if it feels safe, it's very compliant. If it doesn't feel safe, though, it'll flee and be unpredictable. If the rider is communicating well with the horse, giving clear instructions, then reading and receiving signals back from the horse, the pair are in alignment – they become one. However, if the rider is giving certain signals to the horse, like pulling on the reins to turn, but at the same time thinking: 'Last time I went right, something terrible happened and I'm really scared,' the horse receives mixed messages and just stops. It doesn't trust the rider because it's not getting a clean, clear instruction. What this means is, if our thoughts, actions and behaviours aren't aligned it will be apparent and the desired outcome won't be achieved. This reminds us that the clarity and quality of the thinking mind is important, but stress diminishes this clarity – which is why it is so essential that we find ways to de-stress.

– Kay, Farnborough branch, wellbeing specialist and author of
  Happy Brain

Flipping the switch

Hold out your hand with your palm facing upwards.

Fold your thumb inwards. Think of this as the amygdala, the emotional part of your brain, right in the centre, which needs to be protected.

Now fold your fingers down over the top of your thumb to make a fist with the thumb tucked inside. Your fingers represent your prefrontal cortex – the rational, safeguarding part, trying to protect the emotional bit.

Now flip your fingers back up again. This is what a stressed or anxious brain can be like: as if the prefrontal cortex is a switch that has been flipped the wrong way, meaning the whole brain no longer works harmoniously.

In order to flip the switch back down and reconnect the whole brain, let's think of some strategies for feeling safe, calm and connected:

Three thoughts that calm me:

1 . . . .

2 . . . .

3 . . . .

Three emotions I'd like to feel more of:

1 . . . .

2 . . . .

3 . . . .

Three behaviours that help me feel safe, calm and connected

1 . . . .

2 . . . .

3 . . . .

Neuroplasticity

Scientists used to think that the brain didn't develop further after adolescence and couldn't be changed. Neuroplasticity is a recent development that has proved the brain can and does continue to grow throughout our life. It generates new tissue and neurons, and makes different connections all the time. Imagine your brain as a map, with loads of little footpaths that represent a route each time you think, feel or do something. The most well-travelled pathways are our habits, both good and bad. Each time we repeat the habit, we strengthen the pathway.

So, what does this mean for our emotional wellbeing? Well, it means that we have a two-way relationship with our brain, and thus the opportunity to rewire it. Where we used to think that the brain dictates the action, we have come to realise that we can also do the reverse. We can create new neural pathways that rewire the way we think, feel and behave. Everything we experience changes our brains a little bit, and those changes affect how we respond to future stimuli – it's a constant feedback loop. This neuroplasticity (think of it like moulding plastic) gives us the chance to change our habits and, with it, we can hope to improve our mental health.

Try and think of it like this: imagine you're walking down a path. One you walk down all the time and know so well that you follow it automatically. Eventually, the path gets so well-trodden it just naturally becomes the one you always go down. It's completely normal for you to do so.

But what if, when you get to the path you usually go down, you *could* stop and think, 'Actually, I'm going to go this way instead.' At first, the new pathway will be overgrown. It won't be easy – the easiest path to go down is the one you're used to, back that way… But, in time, if you keep trying the new route, the way will become clear, and you will find it's just as easy as the old one. In terms of neuroplasticity, the brain is now all set to use the new pathway – and if you keep using it it will make it stronger still. Eventually, it will become second nature as the old pathway weakens. The new pathway may be a new way of thinking or of behaving that could alter and improve the way you feel.

PATHWAYS

Draw a pathway, one that feels very familiar to you, that you might usually choose to go down.

Now imagine a new pathway for yourself, one that you could choose to go down as an alternative. If you could draw a new pathway – what would that look like to you? What detail would there be?

Have a look at what you've drawn. What do you recognise? Does any of the imagery strike a chord within you? Note down any thoughts or feelings.

. . . .

. . . .

. . . .

Communication and connection

'Our thoughts are all real, but they're not necessarily true. You can't deny them, so it's important to try and help people understand what they represent.

I studied interpersonal neurobiology and realised that whatever comes out in people's emotional response is a valid reaction, and that what's important is helping people work on their connection to each other, which is very similar to what we do at Samaritans.'

The inner conversation is no different from the outer one. One approach is that you begin with self-compassion and work outwards – which is kind of the opposite of what we've been taught to believe. The concept of putting ourselves first is very alien to us, but it's so important. People who contact Samaritans often don't have the tools for being kind to themselves. We all know the phrase 'Treat others as you would treat yourself,' but for me, I tend to think, 'Treat others the way a Samaritan would treat someone who was asking to be heard.'

A lot of it is about trying to untrain ourselves from social conditioning. But it's also about learning more of an emotional vocabulary, and giving a name to our feelings and our emotions. If you can work out your 'mood meter' – what it might mean when you're feeling angry or excited, sad or joyful, numb or calm – you will be able to understand more about your own emotional states as well as recognise these emotional states in others.

Both neuroscience and mindfulness have a lot to offer, and both have become very popular, and therefore populist. It's important to choose what works best for you. What makes one person feel comfortable or comforted might make someone else feel threatened or afraid – or could even open up something that they can't deal with alone. What's important is to understand how best to articulate what's going on, and then know that it's OK to deal with it in your own way, and that self-care means talking about what you're going through. In itself, the right diagnosis and the right treatment can be a form of self-care, as well as speaking to someone you know, or speaking with a professional and getting the support you need.

– Ian, Hastings and Rother branch, and author of
If It Is So Good To Talk, Why Is It So Hard?

The difference between thoughts, feelings and behaviours

In psychology, there is something called the 'Cognitive Model', which details a process that looks something like this:

Something happens > My brain thinks a thought about the thing that happened > This creates an emotional response > The emotional response affects my behaviour.

| SITUATION | > | THOUGHT | > | FEELING | > | REACTION |

| Something happens | My brain interprets what happens | I have an emotional response to the thought | I have a physical response to the emotion |

If you want to, have a think about how this might apply to you. Have you ever noticed that in a specific situation, you respond in a certain way? Write down a few words or sentences about how you might have reacted in a particular moment that you can remember. Then, working backwards, try to think about what was happening emotionally for you at that time. What were your thoughts like in the moment? Jot down any memories or recollections about your thought process.

In a specific situation, such as . . . .

I think . . . .

I feel . . . .

I behave . . . .

Why do you think this might happen?

. . . .

. . . .

. . . .

Would you like to react differently in future?

. . . .

. . . .

. . . .

How do you think you might be able to do that?

. . . .

. . . .

. . . .

What do my thoughts and behaviours look like?

EMOTION	THOUGHTS	BEHAVIOURS
Anger		
Sadness		
Happiness		
Surprise		
Disgust		
Fear		

Behaviours

- Isolating myself from others
- Being snappy
- Getting overexcited
- Overeating
- Being short of patience
- Being stroppy
- Low sex drive

- Being full of nervous energy
- Walking away
- Confronting the situation
- Withdrawing
- High sex drive
- Not eating

Thoughts

- **Overthinking** – imagining every possible outcome.
- **Positive thinking** – imagining the best possible outcome.
- **Ruminating** – thoughts running round and round like a loop in my head.
- **Mind chatter** – continual noisy thoughts running through my brain.
- **Selective thinking** – focusing on one small detail without looking at the bigger picture.
- **Polarised thinking** – a 'black and white' way of thinking. with no in between.
- **Catastrophising** – imagining the worst possible outcome.
- **Assuming responsibility** – taking on too much responsibility, even when something is outside of my control.
- **Problem-solving** – trying to work out the issue.
- **Magnifying** – making problems seem bigger than they really are.
- **Perfectionism** – having impossibly high standards.
- **Sensitive thinking** – taking things too personally.
- **Minimising** – downplaying important things.
- **Personalising** – thinking things are my fault even though there's no possible way they could be.
- **Generalising** – making sweeping conclusions based on one small event.

THE WAY I THINK

When I think. . . . .

I feel. . . . .

. . . .

. . . .

When I think. . . . .

I feel. . . . .

. . . .

. . . .

When I think. . . . .

I feel. . . . .

. . . .

. . . .

When I think. . . . .

I feel. . . . .

. . . .

. . . .

THE WAY I BEHAVE

When I feel. . . . .

My behaviours are. . . . .

. . . .

. . . .

When I feel. . . . .

My behaviours are. . . . .

. . . .

. . . .

When I feel. . . . .

My behaviours are. . . . .

. . . .

. . . .

When I feel. . . . .

My behaviours are. . . . .

. . . .

. . . .

Behaviours to look out for

It's important to be aware of changes in our behaviour in case this means something about our emotional state. Think of the things you might look out for in friends that would cause concern – different eating patterns, not turning up for work, not going out as much as they usually do, using drugs or alcohol excessively, or not communicating with friends and family. In the same way you might ask that friend, 'You don't quite seem yourself at the moment, are you OK?' make sure you take the time to ask yourself the same thing. Signs and behaviours that may indicate you're experiencing emotional difficulties could include:

- lacking energy or feeling particularly tired
- feeling irritable, restless and agitated
- being more tearful than usual
- not wanting to talk to or be with people
- not wanting to do things you usually enjoy
- changing your routines, such as sleeping or eating more or less than normal
- using alcohol or drugs to cope with feelings
- finding it hard to cope with everyday things
- not liking or taking care of yourself, or feeling as if you don't matter
- being untypically clumsy or accident-prone
- becoming withdrawn or losing touch with friends and family
- not replying to messages, or being distant
- becoming angry, aggressive or defensive
- doing more risky things, or becoming self-destructive

Make a note of any patterns of behaviour that are particular to you that could remind you when it's extra important to use self-empathy and self-compassion.

I will treat myself kindly if I...

. . . .

. . . .

Relaxation exercise

Make yourself as comfortable as possible, whether that's lying down, sitting or standing.

Close your eyes if you can, or keep them open if you'd like.

Take a few slow, deep breaths.

Notice the sensations in different parts of your body.

Bring your awareness to the breath, just recognising how it feels.

Notice what you enjoy – the silence, the stillness, the connection to the breath, your heart beating.

Some people like to imagine a warm light, white or golden, rolling around inside them as they check in on each part of their body.

Start at your heart, then think of the light flowing down through the ribcage, the stomach, the hips, travelling down into the thighs, knees, shins and ankles, washing all the way down to the tips of your toes, before gently travelling back up through the body to the arms.

Imagine the white or gold gently spilling down your arms to your fingers, then back up, past the wrists and elbows, until the calming light rolls back into your shoulders and up through your neck.

Feel it wash over all the different parts of your face and head before travelling back to the heart and bringing awareness back into the whole body.

Feel the weight of your limbs, the softness of your breath. Imagine that all the stress you have been holding has been washed away.

Wiggle your fingers and toes, take a big breath in through your nose, and thank your mind for taking your body on a journey.

Chapter 6

Dealing with change and challenging negative beliefs

Big life changes

Certain situations can affect how you are feeling, particularly when they involve significant change. It's important to check in with yourself and treat yourself kindly if you are experiencing a big shift in your life, as this can cause new and conflicting emotions to arise. More often than not, these times pass, and we pick ourselves up, shake ourselves down and adjust to our new circumstances. Change can bring positive outcomes, such as personal growth and new opportunities. But adjusting to change can be very difficult, and change that's outside our control can cause anxiety and stress. Remember your personal plan (pages 16-17)) and be aware of the support available to you at these times.

A few examples of big life changes are:

• relationship and family problems

• loss, including the loss of a friend or family member through bereavement

• a change in your financial situation

• job-related stress

• moving to a new place

• college or study-related stress

• painful and/or disabling physical illness.

**MAKE A NOTE OF A BIG LIFE CHANGE YOU HAVE EXPERIENCED,
AND EXPLORE YOUR FEELINGS ABOUT IT BELOW:**

. . . .

. . . .

. . . .

HIGHLIGHT

LOWLIGHT

Draw a timeline

Think about some times when you were at your happiest, and also some when you felt at your lowest. Draw the highlights and lowlights on the line below in the order in which they happened, curving up like a hill or dipping below the line. Add dates and descriptions. Then have a think about the peaks – what really mattered to you then? And in the troughs – what made you dissatisfied or unhappy in those times? Think about what might have affected your perception. For example, were you with other people who altered the situation or how you felt about it? It's important to remember here that no one has ever been above the line all the time. Our lives are wiggly lines, going up and down a bit here and there. What's important is to gently begin to realise what your own patterns of behaviour might be.

Loss

' A lot of us will experience loss of some kind in our lives. When we think of loss, we tend to think of someone dying, which, as we know, is heartbreaking and confusing. But we forget to think about other kinds of loss: loss of security, health or faith; financial losses, or those that can occur in a career. All of these can affect our sense of self and our purpose, and lead to a loss of identity. This has been exacerbated recently by Covid, which has led to many people having to face loss, and at a time when social and emotional contact has been restricted. In some circumstances, such as a loss of health, work or identity, we often don't recognise that what we're experiencing is a form of bereavement. In the same way as the bereaved, we need a listening ear to accept our experience, as well as empathy and support on the journey.

But there's something important about allowing yourself to *feel* loss. About three or four years ago, I entered a spiral of losing my health, my work and my finances. I had to rewrite my own journey, work out who I was all over again, and figure out where I was going. I had to be really aware of the way I spoke to myself during that process. I found that sometimes people gave advice that was well-meaning, but seemed so far removed from my experience of how I was feeling. They would say things like, 'I'm sure everything will be better soon,' which was frustrating, because inside I was thinking, 'Really? How do you know?' Now, when I'm talking to someone at Samaritans, I say, 'I hope things get better for you,' or 'I hope you find your way through this,' and people always say, 'Thank you so much'. It's a small difference, but that distinction between hoping rather than presuming is a really important one.

Whatever it is you're going through, no matter how big or small, it can feel alien or uncomfortable to take the time to say, 'I'm doing OK' – particularly if it's a long way from where you feel like you should be. If it's hard to get up in the morning, acknowledge that. Tell yourself it's OK to feel the way you feel. Accept that this is how it feels for you in this moment, and that that is absolutely fine. However you feel, it's OK to feel that way. Once you've accepted this is what it is, and you are who you are, and what you are feeling is what you are feeling, you might then feel more able to get out of bed. You might want to take a shower. You might then want to go back to bed, but hey – you got up. You had a shower. Those small steps are an achievement, and you can recognise them as such. Tomorrow you might get up, have a shower, and go outside.

Mindfulness (see pages 127–9) can really help when you're experiencing loss, because it's about living in the here and now. We can become attached to ideas of how things 'should' be, and that almost taints the present moment, as if our beliefs own us rather than the other way around. It can mean that we lose the sense of pleasure or gratitude that might exist in that moment. Being mindful is about trying to be aware of your surroundings and absorbed in them, trying to home in on all your senses so that you're aware of what's around you. You can feel really immersed in it, really connected. It's more of a *being* rather than a *doing* thing. You can let go of your attachment to ideas and thoughts and work towards accepting things as they are.

Start small. Put one foot in front the other. Acknowledge your achievements, no matter how insignificant they might seem. Validate yourself and tell yourself it's OK if you found this difficult, then reward yourself for getting through it. Be a friend to yourself, not an enemy. Be kind, be firm when you need to be, and speak to yourself respectfully. Ask yourself, 'What have I done well today?' Even if it was something small, like making a phone call or going out shopping, congratulate yourself. Remember: this is your journey.

– **Heidi, Blackburn branch**

THINKING ABOUT LOSS

What have you lost?

. . . .

. . . .

What do you miss the most?

. . . .

. . . .

How has loss affected you?

. . . .

. . . .

What can you do to help you cope with loss?

. . . .

. . . .

What have you learned about yourself through suffering loss?

. . . .

. . . .

What do you think can help you heal?

. . . .

. . . .

Accept or change?

All of us feel emotional pain, stress, anxiety or uncertainty at some time in our life. Sometimes we can take steps to change our circumstances. Sometimes things are outside of our control. Learning to accept the things that we cannot change can help reduce the suffering that we feel. Accepting something doesn't mean you agree with it, or that it was right. It simply means you acknowledge that it has happened and then try to move on. Learning to accept something that is holding you back takes practice, and you may not be able to do this straight away. It's worth practising this technique, though, as you *can* get better at it.

To get the most out of this exercise, spend as much time as you can writing down what's troubling you. You can then go through and pick out individual issues and sort them into things you can change and things you can't. Once that's done, you can make a plan to change what you can. You'll finish up by learning a little bit about what acceptance means and how to practise it, as well as writing some coping statements.

Try writing down everything you can think of that's bothering you in the space below or on a separate piece of paper. This might be an area of your life you know is causing you pain or negative feelings. For example, you might write 'family', 'money' or 'health'. Try to list as many things as you can. There's nothing too big or small.

* . . . .

* . . . .

* . . . .

* . . . .

* . . . .

* . . . .

Individual issues

Now, try and pick out the individual issues that are upsetting you within those areas. For example, if you've listed 'money', an individual issue might be 'I'm overdrawn' or 'I can't pay rent this month'.

* ....

* ....

* ....

* ....

* ....

* ....

Well done – identifying what's causing our pain isn't always easy. Now, identify the things in the list that you know you're definitely *not* able to do anything about. For example, a bereavement or loss is something that we are not able to go back and change. Next, identify the things that it might be in your power to change. If you haven't identified anything you're able to change this time, feel free to skip this part.

Take some time now to think about what action you can take for each issue. When you're ready, write down your ideas: specific, do-able actions are best. They don't have to be big or drastic. For example, if you've identified loneliness and lack of close friendships as something that is causing you pain, you might write something like, 'Text Jenny and see if she wants to hang out next week'.

Actions I can take

* . . . .

* . . . .

* . . . .

Well done! You've thought of ways to change things that are troubling you and that can be hard to do. It can be helpful to break each action down into manageable steps and think about how and when you might do them. Now move on to the other things on your list.

. . . .

. . . .

. . . .

'A problem is a chance for you to do your best'

– DUKE ELLINGTON

Acceptance

When we're not able to change something that is troubling us, practising acceptance can be a powerful tool to help reduce suffering. For most people, self-acceptance doesn't come easily, but it can be learned and practised. Here are some tips and strategies for practising acceptance.

- Try not to judge what you're feeling as positive or negative – you only need to accept that it has happened.

- Try to think about these things when you are feeling relaxed. You could try using a relaxation technique (such as the one on page 15) or do a relaxing activity beforehand.

- Allow yourself to fully feel any emotions that arise. It's OK to feel sad or angry when trying to accept something difficult. Allow your emotions to pass in their own time.

- Remember, by accepting that something has happened, you are not validating it or agreeing with it. You are being kind to yourself and giving yourself permission by allowing yourself to move on from it.

Coping statements

Coping statements are words to yourself that recognise what you're feeling and emphasise your resilience – these can be helpful when building acceptance. You can use them if you notice yourself fighting something you can't control. For example:

'This is upsetting, but the feeling will pass eventually.'

'I don't have to let this bother me.'

'I've felt this way before, and I'm still here.'

If you would like to, you can use this space to write down some of your own statements here:

* ....

* ....

* ....

* ....

Remember, learning acceptance can take practice and time. It's a process, not something that happens instantly. So don't worry if you haven't got there just yet.

Problem-solving

When you're faced with several problems to try and solve, it can be very overwhelming. Have a think about something that might be troubling you. Remember that not all problems *can* be solved. If you're not sure whether a problem could feasibly be solved, it might help to try using the 'Accept or change?' exercise on page 85.

To begin with, describe the problem you've chosen to work through. This might be an issue that you're having with family or friends, at work, or regarding your financial or living situation. (To get the most out of this technique, you might benefit from practising it a few times with less complex problems.)

Describe the problem as fully as you can:

....

....

....

If you're ready, use the space below to describe how the problem makes you feel. For example, you might feel angry, sad, overwhelmed or something else.

How does this make you feel?
It makes me feel...

. . . .

. . . .

Think about how this became a problem. Sometimes our problems start with a particular event or change. Identifying the time in your life that the problem started can be helpful.

How did this become a problem?
It all started when...

. . . .

. . . .

How would you like things to be different? If you can, describe the best realistic outcome.

For example, this could be a repaired relationship or safety from a fear or threat.

What would be the best realistic outcome?
I'd feel better if...

. . . .

. . . .

If you feel able to, summarise some of the main points you can identify:

. . . .

. . . .

. . . .

Notes:

. . . .

. . . .

. . . .

. . . .

. . . .

. . . .

. . . .

. . . .

. . . .

. . . .

. . . .

. . . .

Control

❝ Sometimes, people have a tendency to blame themselves and feel guilty about or accountable for things that are outside of their control. They might think, 'Why couldn't I stop that from happening?' or 'I should have anticipated something/planned for it/reacted differently to it/done more/done better.' They set themselves impossible standards that, in reality, are unachievable, which means they will always fall short.

There will be some moments in life when your resilience is going to be much higher than at others. Think back to the emotional health scale (page 30). When you're at the top, try to recognise that and think about what helps you be the best version of you so that you can remind yourself that person exists when you're finding it harder to manage.

Often, it comes down to feeling like you are in control or able to influence what is going on. When we get wrapped up in feelings of helplessness, we can lose our sense of control over our own circumstances, and this can exacerbate negative feelings like anger and frustration. It's important to recognise what *is* within our control and what *is not*, and to reframe our thinking accordingly.

In Samaritans training, we recognise the fact that everybody is on a continuum, where their ability to cope depends on the life events they are experiencing. We need to identify and use some constructive strategies and practical steps to help us get through the times that are tough. Ask yourself: what is going to help me cope, both physically and emotionally? It might be really simple things, like sleep, eating, self-care and kindness; it might be trying to cancel out your mind chatter, or reframe negative self-talk. It can also be helpful to talk to someone or get into the practice of writing things down, just to externalise the issue. It's important to try not to self-blame, and to separate the external forces from how they're making you feel.

Reframing techniques can help change negative self-talk into more positive, constructive statements. This can also help you understand that you can't control what's happening around you, but that, over time, you can learn to control your reactions. ❞

– Vanessa, Samaritans Central Office

MAKE A LIST OF THINGS YOU CAN'T CONTROL
For example, other people, technical issues, work incidents.

* ....

* ....

* ....

* ....

* ....

MAKE A LIST OF THINGS YOU *CAN* CONTROL
For example, my choices, my thoughts, my words, my actions and reactions.

* ....

* ....

* ....

* ....

* ....

HOW DO YOU SEE YOURSELF?

....

....

....

....

HOW DO OTHERS SEE YOU?

. . . .

. . . .

. . . .

LIST THREE OF YOUR BEST ATTRIBUTES

1 . . . .

2 . . . .

3 . . . .

Challenging negative beliefs

Sometimes we believe negative things about ourselves without questioning them. Over time, these beliefs can lower our self-esteem. This exercise will help you challenge unhelpful beliefs you hold about yourself by identifying real evidence against these beliefs.

For this to work well, you might need to take some time to think of negative things you believe to be true of yourself. You'll then need to remember to write down a new piece of evidence against your negative beliefs every time you encounter one. For example, if you believe you are lazy, you might note down a piece of evidence about times when you've done something active or difficult.

OK, let's get started. Try to focus on one negative thing you think about yourself. You may find this challenging, so remember you can always pause the technique and come back later. Flip to the beginning of the book to remind yourself of the breathing, relaxation and visualisation tools if you need to (pages 12–15).

One negative thing I believe about myself is:

. . . .

. . . .

. . . .

How much do you believe this at the moment?

Not at all   1   2   3   4   5   6   7   8   9   10   Totally

Why do you think you believe this about yourself?

. . . .

. . . .

. . . .

Every time something happens that makes you believe the negative thing slightly less, write it down here:

. . . .

. . . .

. . . .

Challenging negative self-talk

Try and reframe some of your thoughts. Have a think about some of the ways in which you 'talk' to yourself, then flip them around to make them more positive in tone. The first few have been filled in to demonstrate the idea.

NEGATIVE THOUGHT	REFRAMED POSITIVE THOUGHT
I am not good enough.	I did a good job under difficult circumstances.
I should have done more/I should have done it differently/better	I did all I could in unforeseen circumstances.
I am useless.	I am strong and capable but this was a tough situation and it was OK to ask for help.
I am to blame.	I am not responsible for others' actions and decisions.

Reframing your thoughts and your words when speaking to others

This reframing approach can also work when you're communicating with others. Sometimes it's difficult to communicate exactly what it is going on inside us, and we can fall back into patterns that might not be helpful. For example, have you ever noticed how your instinctive reaction is to say sorry, even when you aren't in the wrong? Take some time to think about how you might be able to reframe particular thought patterns, focusing on what you truly want to convey rather than what you might naturally say. For example, instead of saying, 'I'm sorry for talking so much,' you could say, 'Thank you for listening to me.' When we're feeling upset or struggling to express ourselves, that can sometimes come out as frustration with the person we are talking to, which isn't helpful – and so by reframing these negative phrases, we can help make the conversation more open and constructive. Here are some ideas of thoughts and words that you could try saying out loud to others. Take a look, then try to come up with some of your own examples of reframing a negative communication into a more positive one.

INSTEAD OF SAYING THIS...	...SAY THIS
Why don't you listen?	I feel unheard.
Can we talk?	Would you mind just listening for a bit?
You're not helping.	I feel like I need some more support.
You don't care.	I don't feel cared for.
Stop being so negative.	It's understandable that you feel negative.
I'm sorry for messing up.	Thank you for being patient with me.

Why talking and connecting with others is good

'I'm in my final year of university, studying counselling and psycho-therapy, and I've been a listening volunteer with Samaritans for almost three years. I became a volunteer quite young, but I love it. It isn't just a job; there is a real sense of community, and what we do is so important.

Going through the Covid pandemic and lockdown was really hard. Everything became online and, while I had great support from my tutors while writing my dissertation on trauma therapy, it was so difficult because I was just staring at a screen all day.

Going to university can be quite hard because it might be the first time you go away and the first time you might experience loneliness. There's a pressure to be out having loads of fun all the time, but it's not really the way it's portrayed in the movies or in books. I remember my first day: I was just so nervous. I was worried about making friends and fitting in with the group. Then, when it all comes to an end, you worry about well, what will I do now? For me, it's been really helpful to discuss all the options available and work out which routes I could take. Anxiety can overshadow your thoughts, but when you realise you have different options and there are different paths there, you start to feel more hopeful. It's important to acknowledge how you're feeling so that you can think logically. It can really help to make a list of all the options open to you.

There's such a high rate of loneliness in young people, but it's something we're kind of scared to admit to, because you might think, 'I have so many friends or family members around; I shouldn't really be feeling this way.' But if we were braver about acknowledging it, we would learn to realise it can get better. It's important to realise that it's OK not to be OK.

Now, more than ever, we need to talk about our feelings, and where we're at. We get so used to keeping our emotions in and bottling it all up, but it's OK to speak them out loud. And it's OK to get help. A lot of people call Samaritans because it's anonymous and they don't want to burden people they know with what they're going through. But whether you talk to us or your friends, or journal about your experience, what's important is acknowledging your thoughts and your feelings.

– Aisha, Blackburn branch, psychology student

TRY AND THINK OF ONE SIGNIFICANT LIFE EXPERIENCE –
PERHAPS IT'S GOING TO UNIVERSITY, STARTING A NEW JOB,
MOVING HOUSE OR BEGINNING A NEW RELATIONSHIP.

Describe it below.

. . . .

. . . .

. . . .

What are your main worries?

. . . .

. . . .

. . . .

What are the options available to you?

. . . .

. . . .

. . . .

Who can you talk to about the different options?

. . . .

. . . .

. . . .

ROSE PETAL EXERCISE

Write the positive words into the petals of the rose. You might like to colour in the layers too.

Write some of the perceptions you'd like to leave behind on the rose petals that have fallen off the flower.

What kind of person are you?

. . . .

. . . .

What makes you *you*?

. . . .

. . . .

What is your place in the world?

. . . .

. . . .

What are your best qualities?

. . . .

. . . .

What are the most negative things you think someone could say about you?

. . . .

. . . .

What are the most positive things you think someone could say about you?

. . . .

. . . .

'Don't compromise yourself.
You are all you've got.
There is no yesterday, no tomorrow,
it's all the same day'

– JANIS JOPLIN

IMAGINE YOURSELF AS AN ANIMAL. THINK ABOUT THE QUESTIONS BELOW AND MAKE SOME NOTES OR SKETCH SOME IDEAS.

What animal would you be?

Where would you live?

Why would you live there?

What would make you happy?

What would you need the most?

Reflect on what you've created. Does anything correspond to an area of your own life that might need more nurturing?

Chapter 7
Exploring emotional wellbeing

The problem with definitions

At Samaritans, we often hear people say that they didn't understand what was going on when they were experiencing emotional difficulties. A lot of people will describe how they wished someone had sat them down and said, 'Just in case it ever happens to you, this is what depression/stress/anxiety feels like.' But, of course, it's an almost impossible task, because mental health looks entirely different to different people – it's a totally unique experience based on a zillion factors, all related specifically to *you*.

I have heard someone say that they didn't realise they were depressed because they didn't feel sad – they felt numb. Someone else described it as seeing that the sun was shining but they couldn't feel the heat. I've heard a lot of people say the first time they experienced a panic attack, they felt as if they were having a heart attack, and I've heard others say the way their brain was behaving made them feel like they were 'going mad'. While all of this is valid and true to that particular person at that particular moment, it's never going to be the same for everybody – there is no 'one size fits all' in emotional wellbeing.

Hindsight is a wonderful thing and reflecting on and sharing our past experiences is important. But what feels like low mood to one person might blur into depression for another. One person experiencing stress might have similar symptoms to someone else experiencing burnout. Some people like labels, some don't. Some people find a diagnosis disempowering, whereas others find it helpful to learn more about a specific condition or find the right treatment for them.

Just as Samaritans don't give advice or tell you what it is you're dealing with, this is not a place to diagnose or try to fix or probe into difficult feelings that really need to be worked through with a specialist. But this is a place to look at what's going on for you, where you can work out where you are on the emotional health scale (page 30), and then figure out whether you are able to find a balance or if you feel you are sliding too far down the scale and need to reach out for help. So, let's use this space to explore a few different aspects of mental-health issues that are extremely common. If you are able to learn more about them, you might be more aware of when it's time to reach out for help.

In particular, we're going to think about anxiety, depression and stress. You might want to talk this through with someone you trust, or use the internet or books to read up a little more on the topics. Use the prompts over the next few pages to write some notes about your understanding of these areas. If you're not sure, you can do a little research or come back to this section at another point after you've read more of the book.

Anxiety

Have I ever experienced anxiety?

. . . .

. . . .

How intense have these feelings been?

Manageable 1 2 3 4 5 6 7 8 9 10 Very intense

How often do I feel anxious or afraid?

. . . .

. . . .

When I am anxious, I think:

. . . .

. . . .

When I am anxious, I feel (physically):

. . . .

. . . .

When I am anxious, I feel (emotionally):

. . . .

. . . .

Here are some of the ways I can calm myself down in the moment:

. . . .

. . . .

If the feelings continue over time, I will ask for help by:

. . . .

. . . .

. . . .

. . . .

Depression

Have I ever experienced depression?

. . . .

. . . .

How intense have these feelings been?

Manageable   1   2   3   4   5   6   7   8   9   10   Very intense

How often do I feel depressed?

. . . .

. . . .

When I feel depressed, I think:

. . . .

. . . .

When I am depressed, I feel physically:

. . . .

. . . .

When I am depressed, I feel emotionally:

. . . .

. . . .

Here are some of the ways I can lift myself up in the moment:

. . . .

. . . .

If the feelings continue over time, I will ask for help by:

. . . .

. . . .

Stress

Have I ever experienced stress?

. . . .

. . . .

How intense have these feelings been?

Manageable   1   2   3   4   5   6   7   8   9   10   Very intense

How often do I feel stressed?

. . . .

. . . .

When I experience stress, I think:

. . . .

. . . .

When I experience stress, I feel physically:

. . . .

. . . .

When I experience stress, I feel emotionally:

. . . .

. . . .

Here are some of the ways I can relax and unwind in the moment:

. . . .

. . . .

If the feelings continue over time, I will ask for help by:

. . . .

. . . .

I CAN RELAX BY...

Practising self-care, self-compassion and self-kindness, such as:

. . . .

. . . .

Getting involved with supportive social networks such as:

. . . .

. . . .

Doing my favourite kind of exercise or physical activity, which is:

. . . .

. . . .

Doing my favourite creative activity, which is:

. . . .

. . . .

I can challenge my negative thoughts by:

. . . .

. . . .

I can switch off by:

. . . .

. . . .

Find your happy place

' I had a fairly traumatic childhood and young life, and one of my survival techniques was surrounding myself with colour: expressing myself through any artistic medium, be it painting, drawing, printmaking or sculpture. Colour was and is my language. This, in so many ways, has made me who I am. Art and colour became my toolkit for my own well-being. They helped me get through tough times, and have also helped me with my work as a Samaritan, because I became used to asking, why do I paint what I paint? How does that make me feel?

I have nursed all my working life, but art has been my outlet. It has made me more curious, with a desire to explore and understand. It allows me to work with different mediums and their varying tactile qualities, and to focus on the process of what I'm doing. It can let me forget myself and everything that's been going on, or thoughts about what will happen when I leave the studio, because my headspace is occupied.

I started to run art classes for carers, and now I have become a carer myself; my husband has dementia. Working with art and people is about listening to and supporting others: it's a wonderful way to create a connection. When you're a carer, finding a safe space to be, where you can step into another world for a short time, is of huge importance for your wellbeing. When I walk down to the bottom of the garden to my studio, it is my sanctuary.

You can use art to make your own little sanctuary. You can do it however you want, whether that's decorating an area, hanging a picture, or growing some pot plants on the windowsill. Creativity is about nurture.

When you're faced with a blank sheet of paper, it can be difficult to know where to start. But you can just connect pen to paper and see where it takes you, and that, in itself, is a really great start. Or try just dipping a paintbrush into paint and playing with colour. Charcoal is one of the best mediums to draw with, because it's really smudgy and dirty. You can simply scribble lines with a big chunky piece of charcoal, and then rub it with your hand – which is a nice way of making physical contact with the paper – and then draw into whatever patterns you see. You don't need to plan anything. Afterwards, you can use a rubber to make more patterns, and you've already created something! It's not about the final piece of art: it's what's inside of you that matters.

– Rosie, Taunton branch, artist

Loneliness and isolation

Humans crave attention. We thrive in groups. We are social animals and need other people around us. Feeling connected to others is a basic human need that is essential to our wellbeing. There is a wealth of evidence to show that social connections, whether with a partner, family, friends or work colleagues, can promote good health. Conversely, when we are isolated from others, we can become very unhappy; a lack of supportive relationships or simply a belief that there's no one to turn to can lead to loneliness and, for some, extreme unhappiness and depression.

When we talk about loneliness and isolation, we're not talking about living on a farm in the Outer Hebrides – it can be a feeling as well as a physical thing. You can be very lonely in a relationship if you feel disconnected, or when you're not getting any validation from anybody else. You can feel alone when you're in the middle of a crowd or when you look at social media. That feeling of disconnectedness – *I don't belong, I don't relate, nobody really gets me* – can be exacerbated by social media, as the lives we see presented there are often not real and are viewed – quite literally – through a filter. Technology has given us endless possibilities, but we still need human connection in order to create meaningful relationships. Social-media connections add huge value to our lives, but they can't replace the real thing.

The support we receive makes us more resilient when bad times come along, and that needs to be nurtured. Human connection and the benefits we get from it can help make us better able to cope when there is a crisis, as well as being a safety net for us when we face difficult times. Just being with someone in hard times can be a great support. Our connection with other people – and theirs with us – makes us stronger. When the chips are down, we want to have people around us who care, in whom we can confide and from whom we can get help.

Have you ever felt lonely?

. . . .

What did that feel like?

. . . .

What made you feel better?

. . . .

How can you tell if you need to talk to someone?

. . . .

My support network is...
For example, friends, family members, a support worker, faith group, community group, sports team, Samaritans.

. . . .

Today I will connect with others by...
For example, speaking to someone new, calling a friend, making plans.

. . . .

Today I will connect with myself by...
For example, being honest with myself, trying not to tell myself I shouldn't feel this way, accepting that it's OK to feel the way I feel.

. . . .

. . . .

Overwhelm

' I'll often say to people who contact us, 'It sounds as though you're in overwhelm.' People will talk about several things that feel overwhelming, and any one of these things would be difficult to deal with, but sometimes they all seem to hit at once. And my impression is that multiple things don't just add to what you're already dealing with, they multiply it.

A technique that always helps me is to sit down with a plain sheet of paper and do what I call a 'Worry Dump', where I just write everything down, in no order, with no structure, and no hierarchy or plan. Doing this means I've partly got it out of my system. I don't have to hold it all in my head – it's all there on the paper. I can go back to it whenever I want. And when I feel ready to tackle any of it, I'll look at different points in isolation and think, 'What might I be able to do about that one thing?'

People talk about loneliness or isolation in almost every Samaritans call. Sometimes it can be about a sense of not belonging as much as not being physically around other people. Some people can be lonely even within a relationship, or in a group of people if they feel disconnected.

I have suffered from depression myself, and it's a big, complicated subject. But I have a nice, simple way that I like to look at it that works for me. A lot of the time, we try to bury what's going on. Suppression is when you try to push something to the side, and you know you're doing it. Repression is when you do the same thing, but you *don't* know you're doing it. Either way, it doesn't go away – that's not possible – and that feeling of pushing it all aside creates a real sense of pressure. This pressure builds up inside and can lead to depression.

People may already know the way of expressing their feelings that suits them best, but often it's through words or tears. Tears can help, but we can't always produce them to order, and often men find it harder to express themselves in this way. Whether you say your feelings out loud, write them down or cry them out, these are all ways of expressing them in a way that gets them out of your system.

And don't forget: if you're having a really hard time and it's difficult for you to do something like this alone,
you can call us at any time, day or night. '

– **Joe, Preston and Blackburn branches**

SUPPRESSION, REPRESSION, DEPRESSION, EXPRESSION

What causes pressure for you?

. . . .

. . . .

What does that feel like?

. . . .

. . . .

What are you aware of suppressing?

. . . .

. . . .

Is there anything you think you might be repressing?

. . . .

. . . .

Have you ever felt depressed?

. . . .

How can you express yourself?

. . . .

. . . .

MY WORRY DUMP

Use this page to write out anything going on in your head at this moment. You can come back later and work through different points if you would like to.

. . . .

. . . .

. . . .

. . . .

. . . .

. . . .

. . . .

. . . .

. . . .

. . . .

. . . .

. . . .

CONFUSION

What does confusion feel like to you? Draw a picture of your mind when it feels confused.

Draw a picture of how your mind feels when it's free from confusion.

How might you be able to reframe your thinking about confusion?
For example, 'Confusion is difficult to experience in the moment. But maybe there is a reason behind my confusion.'

. . . .

. . . .

IF YOU COULD THINK ANY THOUGHTS, WITHOUT ANY REPERCUSSIONS OR FEAR OF REPRIMAND, WHAT WOULD YOU THINK? WHO WOULD YOU BE? WHAT WOULD YOU DO? WHAT WOULD YOU FEEL?

. . . .

. . . .

. . . .

. . . .

. . . .

. . . .

. . . .

. . . .

. . . .

. . . .

. . . .

. . . .

'If one has courage, nothing can dim the light that shines from within'

– MAYA ANGELOU

The bigger picture

❛ I've been with Samaritans for just over three years now, and I also work with young people at Birmingham University, helping final-year students with the transition phase from university into work. Post-Covid, people entering the job market are finding it really, really difficult, because the number of people applying for each job has shot through the roof due to redundancies and career changes. I try to help them keep their morale up and talk about the fact that it's OK to feel sad or deflated. I don't tell them to cheer up and that everything is going to be great; instead, I reassure them that it's natural to have a reaction of sadness or stress, or to feel a bit demoralised. That's a normal human reaction to what's going on – it's about how you learn to cope and move forwards that matters.

I encourage them to look at the bigger picture and work on understanding the context of why they're doing what they're doing, and what they want to do next. If they can understand more about their situation, they are more prepared when setbacks come, and they can say, 'It's not the end of the world; these are the reasons why this has happened.'

I didn't get the grades that I needed to get into my first choice of uni, so I decided to keep working in the job I was in and do my degree in psychology with the Open University while working full-time. I think what's important is to work out what your motivation is rather than your end goal. For me, it was that I didn't see many people from an ethnic background in senior roles in the corporate world, and I wanted to change that. It turned out that the weight of my academic success didn't hold as much merit or importance as my actual work experience, but it did give me another skill set. It just shows that there's no right path – there are so many other routes that you can go down. We just need to make informed choices.

It's important to recognise or build your support network, but confidence and self-awareness are key. You can learn to be self-assured enough to realise that if you make a mistake, or something goes wrong, you can learn from it. If you don't learn, then you can't progress.

I try and use a lot of positive reinforcement. People can be so critical of themselves: they often don't balance out the negative way they see themselves with thoughts of how they could look at themselves more positively. When people reflect on and give themselves credit for their good qualities, they stop being so hard on themselves. Nobody's perfect.

It's similar to what we do at Samaritans: we know we're not going to be able to take all the weight off someone's shoulders, but we are able to bear some of it in the time we spend with the person we are listening to. And when they feel like they're facing a huge obstacle, alleviating the burden, can enable them to keep going. ♪

– **Azhar, Stratford-upon-Avon branch, consultant, mentor and psychology graduate**

'We must have perseverance and above all confidence in ourselves. We must believe that we are gifted for something, and that this thing must be attained'

– MARIE CURIE

Self check-in

What am I thinking?

. . . .

. . . .

What am I feeling?

. . . .

. . . .

Can I accept my thoughts and feelings without judgement?

. . . .

. . . .

Can I put a name to my emotions?

. . . .

. . . .

Can I accept those emotions without self-judgement?

. . . .

PAY YOURSELF A COMPLIMENT:

. . . .

. . . .

FAILURE

Do you ever worry about failure? Make some notes below.

. . . .

. . . .

. . . .

Have you ever seen this acronym before?

F – first

A – attempt

I – in

L – learning

Do you think you could switch your thoughts around and see the things you might feel you failed at as learning opportunities? Make some notes about them below.

. . . .

. . . .

MY BEST QUALITIES ARE:

. . . .

. . . .

Chapter 7

Therapy, mindfulness and breathing

The kinds of therapy available

Later in this chapter, we'll be talking about meditation, mindfulness and breathing exercises, all of which can help you learn to become more aware of your thought processes, and we'll be looking at good habits of self-care that can help keep you balanced. But sometimes when there's something more significant going on, or you find that feelings are escalating or patterns of behaviour are intensifying, it's important to get the right kind of help. Here is a list of some of the kinds of therapy that exist. Use this space to research some of them and make notes so that you're aware of the options available to you should you ever need them.

Counselling
Having guided conversations to help you understand how you are feeling and how to deal with those feelings, often in specific areas, such as grief, relationship issues, or big life changes.

Cognitive Behavioural Therapy (CBT)
CBT focuses on the present rather than looking back at your past. It looks at thoughts, behaviours, physical reactions and emotions, and helps you train yourself to accept and change them.

Psychoanalysis
A series of theories and therapies associated with Sigmund Freud. Psycho-analysis brings together the unconscious and conscious parts of the mind to uncover fear or conflict that might have been repressed, particularly in childhood.

Third-wave therapy

This brings together psychological and holistic practices that work towards the idea that, rather than counter or contradict your negative thoughts to try and get rid of them, you can change your relationship with your thoughts so that you can watch them come and go.

Exposure therapy

A specific type of CBT used to treat anxiety disorders. This involves exposing the person to the source of their fear with the intent of revealing whether the danger is real.

Human givens therapy

A holistic and scientific framework based on the fundamental set of needs that come with being human, for example meaning, connection, control, privacy and freedom.

Gestalt therapy

This looks at sensations within the self in the present moment in relation to the environment around us to help us understand our place within the world. It also explores past conflict resolution.

Humanistic therapy

This looks at how to make the best choices for you so that you can be the best version of yourself in the present. It's based on principles of growth and self-development.

Inter-personal therapy

This focuses on your relationships with others and attachment issues.

Mindfulness-based therapy

A form of psychotherapy that brings together psychology, mindfulness, meditation and CBT.

Metacognitive therapy

This focuses changing the *way* people think rather than their actual thoughts.

What is mindfulness?

There are different kinds of spiritual and meditative mindful practices. But put simply, mindfulness is the distinction between the mind dwelling on the past or being concerned by the future, and paying attention to what's happening right now.

The key principle of mindfulness is being aware of yourself and your surroundings – noticing what you are doing and how you are doing it. It's about training the brain and the body to be more aware of what's currently going on, and working towards bringing your focus to the present moment, whatever it is you are doing – whether that's eating, walking or listening to someone. It might involve sitting with a cup of tea and watching the steam rise, focusing attention on your breath, or using your senses to focus on something like a candle or a flower, so that when your thoughts go wandering off somewhere, you have a focal point to bring them back to.

It sounds simple, but the habit of mindfulness takes practice: it means training your mind to always come back to the here and now, gently pulling your attention back to the present moment.

Have a think about how you could pay attention to the present moment – the thoughts, sounds and physical sensations happening all the time that we so often miss. When your mind starts to wander to your to-do list, or what you need to get for dinner, or what you plan to do tomorrow, try to redirect your thoughts back to the here and now.

Today I will be practise mindfulness by…
For example, putting some time in my calendar to go for a walk, taking a lunch/tea break, leaving my phone upstairs, going outside to get some fresh air.

. . . .

. . . .

Mindfulness can help

‘ Any therapy where you're sitting with someone else, trying to think about what's going on inside you, is a kind of meditative practice, as you are really trying to listen carefully to what's going on underneath the surface. Meditation is not about suppressing thoughts: it's about allowing them to surface without getting attached to them. Often, we're in our heads, worrying about what we've done in the past or what could happen in the future. But our sense of being alive is in the present moment.

Mindfulness is a very simple thing. It's about creating a space for ourselves where we can best relax and notice what's going on inside. It's about stopping and giving ourselves time to just be with ourselves. We all have experiences of it, whether it's playing football or walking the dog – times when we can let everything go and just *be*, where we suddenly feel that we are in the moment. Mindfulness can help us stop and think, 'I'm a human being in this body. What is that like? What does it feel like? What's happening in this body?' It's about feeling your feet on the ground, taking a breath, and really experiencing what it means to be an embodied creature.

It's about learning to ask, 'What is it you feel you have to get away from in yourself?' The older we get, the more conditioning we have – being told a certain feeling is bad, or that we're not supposed to feel the way we feel – and that means that when we do have negative feelings, it can cause terrible conflicts in people. And that's where self-compassion comes in.

Some people treat themselves in ways they would never dream of treating other people. They can be very cruel to themselves. Mindfulness can help you catch yourself doing that. There may be good reasons that we feel angry or dislike ourselves, but we tend to repress these until they become an unconscious part of us, because we're afraid of them. We need to treat ourselves with compassion, to be able to say 'Yes, I'm angry, I might have done something I don't like,' but then rather than condemning ourselves, we need to try and understand what's driving this behaviour. When you work through it, there are usually very good reasons for why we're stressed, or angry, or whatever it might be. Meditation can be helpful, as it can help you be still enough to notice what's going on underneath without judgement.

It is important for people to connect with and listen to themselves, but sometimes we need other people to help us see things because we can have real blind spots. I think people can be put off therapy because it's terribly exposing, and we can be afraid of that. People generally only go to therapy when there's a real crisis, or when they start to click that they're stuck in a negative pattern that keeps repeating itself.

Journaling can be incredibly helpful because you're taking time out to sit with yourself. Just the physical act of writing or typing can give you a reflective space to dedicate time to yourself in a structured way. And if it does bring things to the surface, then those things are obviously trying to get out.

I think you can learn to regulate your own emotions, but it takes practice. With anything, whether it's journaling, meditation, mindfulness, or therapy, you've got to put the time and effort in and make it a discipline. In our culture, we often expect a quick fix – we have this idea that things can be bought and solved quickly. But if you've got a difficult problem, it's going to take time and effort
to really understand or resolve it. ♪

– **Paul Salvage, UKCP psychodynamic psychotherapist**

Mantra meditation

Mantra meditation is the practice of focusing on a word that you repeat in your mind for a set amount of time. You might find it useful to practise this type of meditation if you struggle with intrusive thoughts, overwhelming emotions or keeping control of your focus.

Choose something that will have pleasant images and associations, but won't activate other thoughts too much – something like 'cloud', 'flower', 'calm' or 'sky' could work. Once you've found a word you like, stick with it in future sessions.

With mantra meditation, you focus your attention and thoughts simultaneously. This is different from other types of meditation, where you focus your attention on something, like the breath, or where you don't try to focus your attention on anything and just observe what comes up. It's also different from using affirmations, where you repeat a phrase to influence your beliefs. And it's different from visualising, where you try to focus on an image. All you do here is repeat a word and focus on it to the exclusion of everything else.

When you get started, you might find it difficult to just focus on the mantra word. You might find lots of thoughts vying for your attention, and that can make it difficult to work out what you want and need to focus on. By assigning some time to just thinking about your mantra, where you know it is OK not to think about anything else, you can see how the mind tries to bring other things to your attention, even when you don't need it to. It's partly about accepting that your head is going to be full of stimulation that you've picked up from the world – some positive, some negative – and that you might have regrets or unresolved transactions with other people that are playing on your mind. But you can choose to say, 'While I acknowledge all of that, for the next ten minutes, I'm just going to think about this one word, and I'm going to repeat it until there are no other thoughts in my head.'

You can then practise turning your mind back to the thing you want it to focus on. Over time, you'll build this 'muscle' and get better at doing it. If you have an anxious, fearful or agitated mind, practising mantras a lot – and not experiencing a catastrophe while you are doing it – can help your mind learn that it's OK to leave you in control of where to focus. This might help you feel calmer over time.

Your brain might want to throw intrusive thoughts at you, but with practice you can choose to focus on the thing you want to focus on, and you might find your mind becomes more cooperative. Then you can use that power and unity of purpose in other situations, to focus your mind in the direction in which you want it to go.

– **Simon, Samaritans Central Office**

Trying mantra meditation

You don't need to write anything down to do mantra meditation: just choose a word and set aside some time to repeat it. You can use a timer to tell you when to stop; some people use strings of beads instead, repeating their mantra once for each bead.

Connect with nature

Sometimes, going outside and getting some fresh air can really help take our minds off worries and distract us from getting stuck in particular thought patterns. Make time each day to go outside. You might like to engage your senses and make a note of all the things you can see, hear, smell and touch – or even taste, if you get an ice cream or a coffee while out on a walk. Write down your experiences and be as descriptive as you can. Perhaps you could include observations about shapes, colours and other specific details.

Where are you?

* ....

* ....

What can you see?

* ....

* ....

What can you hear?

* ....

* ....

What can you smell?

* ....

* ....

What can you touch?

* . . . .

* . . . .

What can you taste?

* . . . .

* . . . .

'Nature's peace will flow into you as sunshine flows into trees. The winds will blow their own freshness into you, and the storms their energy, while cares will drop off like autumn leaves'

– JOHN MUIR

The waves

If you would like to, you could try using the basic concepts of mindfulness to help with your emotional wellbeing by working towards accepting your thoughts and not being swept away by them. It can be helpful to liken the process to sitting on a beach, acknowledging that the waves will come and the waves will go. If you feel like you're being tumbled around in the current, it's about working out for yourself how to keep your head above water so that you can still see the shore. Feeling trapped in the current can feel so hard. If you're using all your effort on trying to power through it, swimming as hard as you can, but you're not getting anywhere, perhaps it's time to change direction. What happens if you look up, lie on your back and try to float? Can you inflate your lungs like an internal life jacket and breathe out to feel the motion of the waves coming and going? Could you try to focus on the present moment and simply allow the waves to gently drift you back to the shore?

If you can understand what's going on in your brain and recognise what that feels like in your body – for example, 'My heart is beating really fast and I'm sweating, but I know that this is a symptom of panic, and this is the worst it can get' – then you can learn to accept it, and over time, and with practice, to let it go. Remember the process of guiding yourself to a place of peace through questioning, listening, validating, being present in the moment and accepting that whatever it is that you are going through doesn't feel good.

Sometimes in life, you'll find yourself in choppy waters, with high waves and a dangerous current that seems to be pulling you in the wrong direction. And sometimes, you'll be right by the beach where it's nice and warm, and you can paddle around and sit down – you might even be a little bit bored. What we generally try to do is find a happy medium, where you can enjoy a nice swim in the warm, comfortable water, with enough challenge and enough rest to keep you balanced and enjoying the experience.

When you feel panic coming, or depression trying to settle or the red mist of anger rising, learn to ride to the crest of the wave and accept that this is a normal, understandable response, and that it's something you can *recognise* rather than react to. Know that trying to suppress the feeling or fight it is likely to make it worse. It might be hard the first time, but the wave will eventually subside. Perhaps the next one will be smaller. Maybe it'll be bigger, but you'll know the technique to get you through it. The more we practise, the better we will get at predicting the flow of the waves and riding them back to shore.

- Try to accept the emotion as you experience it – imagine that feeling of being in the waves as they rise and fall. You can't control them, but you can help yourself stay afloat.

- Try not to fight against the reaction in your body. The more you try to push it down or block it out, the longer it could last – imagine rising to the crest of the wave and reassure yourself that this will eventually pass.

- Ride the wave of emotion until it dissipates, regulating your breathing, or perhaps counting, as you do so.

- Try not to hold on to the emotion: imagine letting go of it. You can't hold it, just like you can't hold water.

- Count the waves as they come and go.

- Realise that, eventually, the waves stop surging.

Breathing exercises

Anxiety breathing exercise
Take a regular inhale through your nose. Exhale, but for longer. When you exhale, think of it like a balloon deflating. If you would like, and when you're ready, inhale on the count of four. Exhale again, slowly and passively, through your nose. Build up to breathing in for four and out for six.

Breathing for balance
This simply breathing exercise can help with low mood, lethargy, sadness or depression. Breathe in through one nostril while holding the other nostril closed with your thumb or finger, then switch over and breath out through the other nostril. The inhalation can help lift and energise you, and the exhalation is a release that will balance you. Continue for three minutes, with your eyes open or closed – you decide.

Breathing to energise
Lift your arms all the way above your head and breathe in as you do so. If it feels comfortable, feel the corners of your mouth softly curling upwards into a smile. Feel your spine lengthening and the top of your head lifting towards the sky, gently bringing your body into focus. Calmly lower your arms as you breathe out. Repeat this movement as many times as you like.

Box breathing technique
This technique is easy to memorise and can be done almost anywhere. Practise it for as long as you need to. All you need to do is:
1. Breathe in for four seconds.
2. Hold your breath for four seconds.
3. Breathe out for four seconds.
4. Wait for four seconds before breathing in again.

When you practise a breathing exercise, you might find yourself yawning. Don't worry – it's a good thing, because it means you are taking in a lot of oxygen. Try forcing a yawn. See what happens. Try the same for a sigh – breathe in and make a sound when you release the air. As you do, relax your neck, shoulders and any other muscles you're holding tight. Try this a few times.

Why breathing is so important

‘ Everyone wants everything so quickly now – but actually, we need to slow down. We have this window of tolerance, where we exist in the here and now, but if and when there is a perceived threat, we move into a state of hyper-arousal, or a stress state.

Connecting with the self begins with breath work. It can help you find a sense of calm and reassurance quite quickly. Bringing awareness to the breath and focusing on a simple breathing exercise is like giving yourself an internal hug. Biologically, your body has an automatic inbuilt reflex to take an in-breath when you've breathed all the way out. So, if you're in state of high stress and it feels like you are hyperventilating – taking a lot of in-breaths in quick succession – try and concentrate on breathing out for as long as you can, and trust your body to take care of automatically breathing in for you. Keep it simple. Breathing out like this will also reduce your stress or anxiety, because a longer exhalation engages the parasympathetic nervous system (see page 62), and this will help you calm down. The easiest way to make the switch is to breath in for four and out for six. Please refer to pages 12 and 137 for some more examples of breathing exercises.

The other thing you can do if you feel panic rising and adrenaline flooding your system is to burn it off. Your primal fear response is saying ‘Run!’ So, run. Do something active, whether that's doing 20 star jumps or going for a jog. Agree with your brain and work off the adrenaline. Afterwards, your body will be in a state of positive physical exhaustion.

Feeling and accepting the emotions in your body is about movement. Yoga can be very helpful, but you can move in any way that is comfortable for you, whether that's stretching, walking, going for a run, visiting the gym, or something like golf or dancing. When you're anxious, your brain releases high levels of the stress hormones adrenaline and cortisol, but when you move your body, your brain creates natural serotonin – the happy hormone.

Movement can also give your body the sense of physical tiredness that helps with better sleep, which is a more beneficial state than the feeling of stress exhaustion.

When you practise yoga, you activate something called the insula, a part of the brain responsible for regulating the nervous system and immune system. Tapping into that part of you makes you feel like your brain has had a massage.

When we're in a state of distress, rather than thinking with the rational part of the brain, we act and react from the emotional part of the brain, the amygdala, which can mean we feel overwhelmed and unable to reason and think. With breath work and movement over a period of time, we can learn to calm the nervous system and the amygdala. When we are calmer, steadier and feel safe, the thinking part of the brain starts to come back, and we can make better choices.

– **Lorna, UKCP psychotherapist and yoga teacher**

Singing is good for the soul

‘I'm a full-time musician, and a lot of the work I do has a therapeutic element. I work with people in homes, those affected by dementia, people with Alzheimer's and their carers. I use music to relax and distract people.

Music is a very powerful tool for accessing our emotions. It activates the limbic system – the part of our brain that deals with memory and emotion. This is why music is so affecting. Everybody has a soundtrack for their lives, whether they're aware of it or not. There will be songs that come on the radio that remind us of something and can have very strong emotional effects.

Participating in making music as opposed to passively listening can be hugely therapeutic too. Singing is great for things like stress and depression. It's an instrument that everybody can play. It's not about proficiency: it's about joining in and giving it a go. Singing is similar to mindfulness, in that it uses breathwork to slow you down, calm your nervous system and focus your mind. There are lots of physiological benefits to singing – you get more oxygen to your brain and internal organs, because you're forced to take deeper breaths when you're singing long phrases. In the same way that chanting, mantras or meditation can ground and centre you, the repetition of singing can be really comforting. Also, your posture is adjusted, as you naturally sit up straighter. Singing also aids relaxation and better sleep – and it's loads of fun! I have always used it as a way of moderating my emotions. It can be a wonderful tool for changing your mood and lifting yourself out of a situation. It's a great social thing, too – sure, you can do it by yourself, but it's a great way of connecting with others.

Before a performance I do vocal warm-ups to loosen up my body, face and vocal cords. Sometimes I'll make people pull all sorts of silly faces to stretch their facial muscles. We can often hold emotions, such as stress, anger and anxiety, in our jaw and temple area. One way to release that tension is to use a vocal warm-up exercise where you touch every tooth in your mouth with the tip of your tongue. First you go around the inside of your teeth, and then you go around the outside, top row and bottom row. It completely releases those muscles in your neck and jaw that tend to hold tension when you're feeling stressed or anxious.

If you're feeling down, and it's hard to smile, you could use an exercise that engages the same facial muscles you'd use when you smile – it's just practising the vowel sounds but really over-exaggerating them – you need to really stretch and pout. It'll give you a smile without you realising it.

Sometimes you might want to put on some music that makes you feel emotional so that you can just have a good cry and get it all out your system. I call this a 'recreational weep'. When you cry, your body is excreting hormones that you need to get rid of. The chemistry of our tears is different depending on the kind of crying that we do, whether they are tears of grief, anger or physical pain, for example. So, having a good cry can be an enormous release because you might get rid of a lot of the stress hormone cortisol.

– **Edelle, Belfast branch**

MY 'RECREATIONAL WEEP' SOUNDTRACK

Write a list of songs that make you feel emotional that you might use for a 'recreational weep' (as described on page 141).

* . . . .

* . . . .

* . . . .

* . . . .

* . . . .

* . . . .

* . . . .

CREATE A PLAYLIST OF UPLIFTING SONGS

* . . . .

* . . . .

* . . . .

* . . . .

* . . . .

* . . . .

* . . . .

CREATE A PLAYLIST OF COMFORTING SONGS

* ....

* ....

* ....

* ....

* ....

* ....

* ....

CREATE A PLAYLIST OF SONGS WITH CATCHY CHORUSES THAT YOU CAN SING ALONG TO

* ....

* ....

* ....

* ....

* ....

* ....

* ....

Write down the lyrics of a song that you can remember off by heart.

. . . .

. . . .

. . . .

. . . .

. . . .

. . . .

. . . .

Write down the chorus of a catchy song and learn it off by heart. Sing along whenever you hear the song.

. . . .

. . . .

. . . .

. . . .

. . . .

. . . .

. . . .

'Music is the language of the spirit.
It opens the secret of life bringing
peace, abolishing strife'

– ATTRIBUTED TO KAHLIL GIBRAN

Music therapy

' With music, you don't have to use language to communicate – it can help you say what words can't. You don't have to be a musician to take part, and there is no right or wrong way of playing an instrument. It's just about exploring and experimenting.

Music-therapy sessions vary from one to another, but generally it's about sound, it's about music, it's about working with what you are given in that moment. The process is very much about just being able to sit in the present and use sound and instruments to explore emotional states, whether by listening, or playing, or your therapist expressing something in music that resonates with you – it could even be silence. The music is there as a tool for you.

In a psychotherapy session, someone is talking, and someone is listening. But the difference with music therapy is that you can have dialogue and play music concurrently as well as taking turns. If you're expressing something that's really difficult, your therapist can play something that holds you in that space and makes you feel safe so that you can explore further. Music is a great way of getting an emotion out in a positive way – hitting a drum is a safe way of expressing anger, for example.

We all have music within us. There's rhythm in our pulse and breathing; there's melody in our language. Expressions of anger, the way we show our joy – the sounds we make, gasps and sighs, are all very musical. And that's our starting point.

A music-therapy session can be structured or unstructured, depending on the individual and what they want to do. You can do really organised things, like listening to songs together or exploring lyrics, or examining the importance of a particular piece of music that's been important to you in the past. You can play an instrument, or just pick one up and see what happens. It's about seeing what comes out and if there's a meaning behind it: if there's something there that's important to listen to, and to hear. It's about a connection to the sound and connection to something that makes the sound.

There are things you can do by yourself, like singing along to your favourite song, or simply making different sounds in a mindful way to bring you into your body. Try holding your hand on your chest to feel the vibration when you sing deeper or higher. You could make a lyric collage, come up with your own melody or write some lyrics.

Music can help focus you so that you can access your feelings, but it can also help you get to a place where something is released that you didn't know was an issue – it could be that you hadn't realised you were angry, but you start playing an instrument and, all of a sudden, you're there. Whenever emotions become heightened, I go back to the natural rhythm of the breath. There's something special about someone being in the moment: they're not second-guessing anything, they're just being, just feeling what they're feeling.

– Elen Evans, music therapist

Creative therapies

In my work in the therapeutic arts, one of the things I try to do is slow down the thinking – that turmoil in somebody's mind – and give the person time to see those thoughts individually and from a different perspective. Creativity really does that. We use a whole range of different arts, but it's all about giving people a different way to engage, helping them to communicate when they are struggling to do so. In terms of the biology of the brain, this creates connections where there weren't any before.

Creative therapy also acts as a distraction. Doing something creative occupies a different part of the mind from the one that might be suffering. It's about the process rather than the art itself, whether it's painting by numbers, poetry, dance, music, song, collage or textile work. All of it is a mechanism to help the mind engage and think differently.

Creative activities like painting, sketching, crafting and crocheting all give you a result. When you are feeling a little bit demotivated, these activities give you something you can do, and afterwards you will have something to show for it. This can give you that little boost you need to carry on.

The process of creativity uses focus to create a sense of calm. We can see the same thing with listening. When someone is in a state of distress, you can distract and soothe them through allowing them to express whatever it is they want to say. It's about breaking the old connection that corresponds to negative thoughts and feelings, and creating a new one that has a sense of the now, of refocusing, of purpose.

Creativity is a very mindful act in that you have to focus on the present moment and pay close attention to what you're doing, whether that's acting or making puppets. It can also bring communities together through making plays or putting together exhibitions. It gives a reason for people to connect through common interests and experience. Sharing skills with one another acts as a vehicle for communication, and from that initial connection, other reasons to communicate will flow, because people have started engaging with each other.

In one project, we gave people materials with which to make puppets of themselves, and then the puppets told the stories the people found it difficult to tell. This ended not just with people sharing their stories, but actually getting up to tell them in a theatre, with members of the public coming to watch. Something was released during that course of creation that enabled those people to tell their story on a stage and feel comfortable doing that. It was as if they were slightly distanced from the confrontation of talking about how they felt. But equally, it gave each person the power to tell a story in their own way. Being creative releases something inside us that enables us to see everything in a different light. ♪

– Keith, Inverness branch and Creativity in Care practitioner

THE TREE OF YOU

Draw an image of a tree. It can be as simple or as detailed as you would like, but make sure there is as much going on beneath the soil as there is above. Perhaps you could begin by drawing a line across the centre of the page, above which you can draw the trunk of the tree, its branches, its leaves and the sky. Then, below the line, draw the roots of the tree, making them equal in size to the part of the tree that shows above the ground. Perhaps you might like to colour in the tree.

Now, if you want to, you could write words on the branches, leaves or roots. Be aware of describing what's going on above the surface as well as the bits of the tree that people can't see. Think about the sensitivity of the leaves, the strength of the branches, the depth of the roots.

For example, you could write:

- words on the leaves describing how others might see you

- words on the branches describing your best qualities

- words on the trunk describing what keeps you strong

- words on the roots describing what keeps you grounded

- words in the soil describing what makes you feel comfortable

- words in the sky describing how you would like to feel in the future.

As you draw, you might like to try repeating some of these phrases, like the mantra exercise on page 130:

- I can breathe.

- I am strong.

- I am connected.

- I am grounded.

- Some leaves will fall, but others will grow in their place.

- Different seasons bring different challenges.

- I can grow.

- I can keep growing.

Emotional Freedom Technique

' I practise Emotional Freedom Technique (EFT), which is something you can do alongside a practitioner or by yourself. It's a self-tapping exercise that can calm you down in the moment and alleviate the feelings of overwhelm or anxiety that can come alongside stressful thoughts.

When we're in a stressful situation, hormones kick in and trigger the fight-or-flight reaction. Sometimes this can happen when you're simply *thinking* about a stressful situation, whether that's going to the supermarket or getting on public transport, and the adrenaline that floods the system can actually physically impair the body. By tapping on a number of acupressure points – similar to the ones used in acupuncture – you're tapping into the energy system within your body, which helps bring that level of anxiety down so that you can stop, breathe and focus. Think of it like a sensory hack.

When working with someone in practice, I would also talk to them about specific issues while using the tapping technique. In this process, there are three phases: 1) checking in on ourselves; 2) setting up the actual issue; then 3) doing the tapping and ending with a positive. It's easy to do. Let's use the example of needing to take the bus when it's something you find very stressful. The first thing we do is check in on our levels of anxiety, on a scale of one to ten, ten being the most extreme. In the set-up phase, you say the issue out loud three times while tapping the side of your hand (the side where your little finger is). Keep swapping hands about every six taps. So, I would say something like, 'I'm feeling anxious. I'm worrying about getting on the bus and feeling really stressed – I don't want to do it. But even though I'm going on a bus today, and it feels really scary, I completely accept myself. I'm OK.' It's about registering that even though something negative is going on in the body, you are saying, 'I still love myself and I'm going to manage this.' Saying it out loud three times allows you to just focus on the issue and be present with it.

Then we start the tapping phase. What you do is tap quickly on the areas below with your fingers, with as much or as little pressure as you find comfortable. Tap each area about ten times before moving on to the next point:

- inside of one eye, by the bridge of the nose
- outside of one eye
- under the eye along the cheek bone, then swap to the other eye
- under the nose
- the chin
- the collarbone (aim for the little hollow just below the dip of your collarbone, about halfway along, and use your whole palm for this point)
- under the arm, near to the rib cage
- the top of the head.

As we tap, we will then break down the phrase we're working with into little bite-sized pieces and say it out loud, for example:

- inside of the eye – 'feeling anxious'
- outside of the eye – 'feeling really anxious'
- under the eye – 'worrying about getting on the bus'
- under the nose – 'feeling really, really stressed'
- the chin – 'I don't want to do it'
- the collarbone – 'I know I have to do it'
- under the arm – 'I will do it, and I will be OK'
- the top of the head – 'but I might feel anxious when I do it'.

You can repeat this practice with any new words, thoughts or phrases that pop up as you go, and you might continue this for five rounds. Then check in with yourself and measure your sense of anxiety on a scale of one to ten to see if the level has changed. When we're in that fight-or-flight scenario or feeling low, it can be difficult to control ourselves, but by tapping into your energy field, you can help your body to calm down, and begin to look at a situation more logically.

If you're in a public situation and don't feel comfortable doing the tapping exercise above, you can do a similar exercise that involves just tapping on the inside of your fingers. You can do this anywhere as it's very discreet, and it can help you to distract yourself, tap into the energy system and calm down.

It's about allowing yourself to feel what you're going through and acknowledging that it's happening, while getting your mind to focus on something else. Over time, you'll able to connect with the logical side of your brain faster, rather than getting so caught up with the emotional side.

One aspect of EFT is that you have to take part physically and verbally, so your mind is concentrated on the here and now. It's similar to how, at Samaritans, we validate someone's experience, then try gentle questioning to allow them to explore what's going on for them emotionally. Everyone is different, and whatever your issue is, you are feeling it, so therefore it must be real. It's all a journey, and it's important to recognise there's not one set route. There are so many different paths that enable you to see and think more clearly, and you need to find the one that is right for you.

– **Heena, Ealing branch, Emotional Freedom Technique practitioner**

Chapter 8
Hope, habits and boundaries

Having hope

Think about Heidi's story on page 83, where she talked about how it felt better to hear someone say, 'I hope things get better for you', rather than 'I'm sure things will be fine'. Make a list of things like this that you would like someone to say to you, such as 'I hope you find your way through this.'

* . . . .

* . . . .

* . . . .

* . . . .

MAKE A LIST OF THINGS YOU COULD SAY TO YOURSELF, SUCH AS, 'I HOPE I CAN KEEP MOVING FORWARDS.'

* . . . .

* . . . .

* . . . .

* . . . .

I AM GRATEFUL FOR:

* . . . .

* . . . .

* . . . .

* . . . .

I AM HOPEFUL ABOUT:

* . . . .

* . . . .

* . . . .

* . . . .

HOPE COLLAGE
Flick through some magazines, postcards or old books and cut out pictures that represent hope for you. Make a collage out of them.

THINKING ABOUT HABITS

What are your unhealthiest habits?

. . . .

. . . .

How can you stop some of them?

. . . .

. . . .

What are your healthiest habits?

. . . .

. . . .

How can you practise these more often?

. . . .

Habits

'I've been a listening volunteer for about four years and am a mediator and conflict coach. When working with people, I always think, what's the dynamic here? What are this person's obstacles? And where are their traps? But people don't want things done for them: they want to know they're sorting things out themselves. When you speak to someone at Samaritans, you're gently guiding them to talk about how they're feeling, without telling them what to do or giving advice – all the decisions they make are their own. You just give them the freedom to let it all out.

We need to take the same approach to our emotional health as we do our physical health. We can all develop simple practices in our everyday life to help us improve our habits and increase our mental fitness. The principles we use at Samaritans, like compassion, empathy and non-judgement – are all things we can apply to ourselves and use to create good habits of self-care in the way we behave and speak to ourselves.

The more we repeat and reinforce things in our internal dialogue, the stronger they get, together with any patterns of behaviour associated with them. Imagine that the thoughts in your head are like plants in your garden. In order to have a beautiful garden, you need to choose the right plants, taking into consideration all the key factors that determine the best plant for each particular spot. Then you need to take care to water, feed and tend these plants to help them flourish. Weeds need to be pulled out before they gain a hold and sap the energy from the plants you want to cultivate.

Our minds are like our bodies. Recognise what each of them needs to serve us well and take a common-sense, scientific and logical approach to improving your mental diet. We are dynamic beings with the capacity to change. Once we appreciate the consequences of allowing certain thoughts and energies to take root, we are able to stop and decide for ourselves what tools we might need to introduce new habits, which, when repeated on a regular basis, can lead to the changes required for us enjoy a happier, healthier future.

What is most helpful will be completely unique to each person. Imagine you are packing a bag to go on a hike. What would you take with you? What's going to be most useful to you on your journey? What's not so useful? What's going to weigh you down? Then pack your 'brain backpack' and apply the same idea. Write down some notes, draw some of the kit, colour in different parts of the backpack that represent the balance of the load you're carrying. Then, in the evening, review what was crucial on your 'hike', and what wasn't needed. This kind of activity can build a habit of self-reflection that, over time, increases your awareness of what is most useful for your mindset. Think of it like going to the gym – you set the time frame, build your own mental circuit-training routine, and choose which exercises work best for you. It's totally up to you to determine the parts of yourself that need the most attention and care.

– Caroline, Eastbourne branch, mediator and author of *Mental Fitness*

Boundaries and standards

Sometimes we put pressure on ourselves to try and do it all – to be there for others, take on extra responsibilities, do what other people want or expect of us. It's OK to pause occasionally and take stock of whether we're carrying too much and need to drop some of the plates we are spinning.

Personal boundaries are the thoughts, feelings and beliefs that define the parameters of our relationships. It is important to remind yourself and others of what you need in order to feel safe, content and valued – they can include emotional, physical, sexual, mental or financial. Have a think about how you behave with other people. For example, having too few boundaries might mean that you struggle to say no and take on too much. Very rigid boundaries might mean that you find it hard to let others in.

It's OK to set boundaries or standards for ourselves, and others, to explain that in order to stay healthy, we need to adhere to these rules. For example, it's OK to say you don't want to go out and socialise. Or if a friend or family member asks you to take something on – whether emotional, or a task – it's OK to say that, at the moment, you're unable to help. Clear boundaries and standards can also help you recognise when others are or are not respecting your needs, something that is vital in good, balanced relationships. Communicating the things you find acceptable or unacceptable is really good practice for being open, honest and clear with others.

Make a list of boundaries you would like to set for yourself:

* . . . .

* . . . .

* . . . .

* . . . .

Make a list of standards you would like to set for yourself:

* . . . .

* . . . .

* . . . .

* . . . .

Make a list of boundaries you would like to set for others/someone else:

* . . . .

* . . . .

* . . . .

* . . . .

Make a list of standards you would like to set for others/someone else:

* . . . .

* . . . .

* . . . .

* . . . .

Chapter 9
Self-care

What is self-care?

S elf-care will mean different things to different people. For some, it's about building good habits into our basic routines, like making sure that we eat, sleep, exercise and think well. For others, it will be about calming the body and mind through things like yoga, breath work, meditation and mindfulness. It can also mean creativity, education, connecting with others, forgiving yourself, letting go of things that aren't good for you and staying hopeful. It might mean getting the right diagnosis for a condition – mental or physical – and then working out the best route to recovery and healing. Overall, it's about treating yourself in the same way you would treat others – with kindness, empathy and compassion.

Self-care is also part of the longer-term process of understanding how to keep yourself balanced over time, so that if you begin to travel too far down on the emotional health scale (page 30), you will have the tools ready that will enable you to support yourself. These can be things like the long-term practice of mindfulness, meditation and self-awareness to make sure your thoughts are supported, as well as ongoing creative and educational activity, and regular habits of movement and physical fitness. Some people find that keeping to a regular routine can help them create a reassuring sense of order and balance.

Over the next few pages, we will look at some tips and suggestions about how to practise self-care so that you can have a think about what might work best for you.

Be active

The way in which we choose to move our bodies is a very individual thing for each of us. Exercise is essential for wellbeing, and it doesn't need to be particularly intense for you to feel good: slower-paced activities, such as walking, can have the benefit of encouraging social interactions as well as providing a level of fitness. Physical activity of all kinds can release endorphins in the brain that can make us feel good. Have a think about your favourite physical activities – what gets you moving and what works for your lifestyle? Do you think you could build these into a daily or weekly plan? Here are a few ideas for getting physical.

- do some simple stretches

- go swimming

- ride a bike

- go for a walk

- take an exercise class

- try jogging

- do an online fitness tutorial at home

- take a yoga class

- join a gym

- join a local sports group

Notes:

. . . .

. . . .

. . . .

. . . .

. . . .

Nutrition

Whatever and whenever you choose to eat is very personal to you, so take time to reflect on this and think about what the healthiest choices for you would be. Acknowledge that this is a mindful choice on your part, and that you have your own health in mind as you set your intentions. Try to adopt a mindset that reminds you to look after yourself and eat well for your mental health, however that looks for you. Nutrition is important, and you need to put the right kind of fuel in your body to stay well. You need energy to get up and go about your day, and good food to help you sleep better at night. Have a think about your habits and see if there is anything you would like to change.

What are your eating patterns?

. . . .

. . . .

How do you feel about them?

. . . .

. . . .

Is there anything you'd like to change?

. . . .

. . . .

If so, how will you go about making those changes?

. . . .

. . . .

Who can you ask for support?

. . . .

. . . .

How will you feel if you don't totally succeed in making those changes?

. . . .

. . . .

How will you feel if you do succeed?

. . . .

. . . .

How will you ensure you practise self-compassion throughout?

. . . .

Notes:

. . . .

. . . .

. . . .

. . . .

. . . .

Sleep

Getting good rest is like rebooting your computer. We need to recharge so that we can heal. Our bodies repair themselves when we sleep, and our brains process what we've experienced that day. Not sleeping well can leave us feeling foggy, contribute to anxiety and depression, and can even affect our immune system. Think about your sleep patterns and ask yourself if there's anything you'd like to change.

Do you sleep well?

....

How much sleep do you get at night?

....

How much sleep do you think is good for you?

....

What stops you from sleeping well?

....

What do you think might help you sleep better?

....

Notes:

....

....

The emotional sponge

When the weight we're carrying gets too heavy, we need to know how to let some of it go.

Imagine a bath sponge. When it's dry, you can pick it up and it feels light – you can throw it around and drop it, then pick it up again. But put it in the bath and it begins to absorb water. Soon, it is so saturated that it sinks to the bottom – it can't hold any more water, and it's heavy. To make it light again, you can wring out the sponge, release some of the water and then let it dry out.

It's the same with emotions. Sometimes, we can take things on – day-to-day stresses, strains and issues. But when we take on too much, and get waterlogged, we need to find a way of releasing the heaviness, otherwise we will feel as though we're sinking. Have a think about how you 'wring out the sponge': how you recover emotionally when you're feeling down or stressed out. Do you go to the gym to increase your endorphins? Do you call a friend to have a chat and get something off your chest? Do you wrap yourself in a blanket and watch your favourite TV show?

Make a list of some of the ways you could wring out your emotional sponge

* . . . .

* . . . .

* . . . .

* . . . .

* . . . .

* . . . .

Engage the senses

If you're suffering from overwhelm or negative feelings, there are things you can do in the moment that can help change your focus out of a difficult mindset and into a more positive one. Think of it like a sensory switch that might interrupt chaotic or noisy thoughts or loops of negative self-talk. To snap the synapses out of a certain way of thinking, focus on something positive or soothing in the moment so you can begin to relax. For example:

- have a cup of tea

- light a scented candle

- take a warm bubble bath

- wrap up in a cosy blanket

- watch your favourite film or TV show

- make yourself some food

- try practising a mantra (see page 130)

- listen to some music

- use some essential oils for a massage or aromatherapy

- have a change of scene – go outside, to the shops, to a park or for a drive

- go outside and get some fresh air.

Add some of your own ideas for engaging the senses

* . . . .

* . . . .

* . . . .

* . . . .

* . . . .

Take some time to enjoy the moment and the environment around you

Being aware of what is taking place in the present directly enhances your wellbeing, and savouring the moment can help to reaffirm your priorities. Heightened awareness also enhances self-understanding and allows you to make positive choices based on your own values and motivations. Here are a few ideas to try:

- switch off your phone for a while

- have a 'clear the clutter' day

- visit a new café for lunch

- take notice of how your friends, family, loved ones and colleagues are feeling or behaving

- practise mindfulness

- get a plant

- go outside and be in nature

- go for a walk

- look at the view from the window or an image in a book and pay close attention to it, noticing all the small details.

Add some of your own ideas for enjoying the moment and your surroundings

* . . . .

* . . . .

* . . . .

* . . . .

* . . . .

Learn

Continued learning throughout life enhances self-esteem and encourages social interaction and a more active lifestyle. The practice of setting goals is strongly associated with higher levels of wellbeing. Why not learn something new today? For example:

- try out a new recipe

- sign up for a class

- practise meditation

- read the news, a book or a magazine

- do a crossword or sudoku

- learn to play an instrument

- research something you've always wondered about

- learn a new word

- watch an interesting documentary

- learn the lyrics or the tune of a song.

Add some of your own ideas for ways to learn

* . . . .

* . . . .

* . . . .

* . . . .

* . . . .

* . . . .

* . . . .

* . . . .

Give

Participation in social and community life can be great for wellbeing. Giving back and performing an act of kindness can really improve our mood.

- smile at a stranger

- become a volunteer

- cook a meal and take it to a friend

- donate to a charity shop

- visit an elderly neighbour

- make a gift for someone.

Add some of your own ideas for ways to give

* ....

* ....

* ....

* ....

* ....

* ....

* ....

* ....

Connect with others

Feeling close to and valued by other people is a fundamental human need, and one that contributes to emotional wellbeing. So take the time to connect with friends, loved ones, family members, colleagues and neighbours. You can do this at work, at home, in school or as part of your local community.

• arrange to see a friend

• talk to someone instead of sending an email

• call a family member

• speak to someone new

• ask how someone's weekend or day was, and really listen to what they tell you

• join a community group

• give a colleague a lift to work or share the journey home with them.

Add some of your own ideas for connecting with others

✻ . . . .

✻ . . . .

✻ . . . .

✻ . . . .

✻ . . . .

Creativity

Doing something creative is a fun way of really focusing the mind and concentrating, as well as doing something tactile with your hands, which can bring the brain and the body into balance. It stimulates the senses, like sight and touch, and releases dopamine, a chemical in the brain that helps us feel pleasure. Working towards a finished piece can also give us a sense of purpose.

- cook or bake something challenging

- draw or paint something

- make a themed playlist

- do a jigsaw puzzle

- do some mindful colouring

- try writing a poem or a short story

- do some journaling or scrap-booking

- try an online craft tutorial

- sign up to a regular class or course.

Add some of your own ideas for getting creative

* . . . .

* . . . .

* . . . .

* . . . .

* . . . .

* . . . .

Hygiene and order

Sorting out the space around us can be helpful for both physical and emotional wellbeing. Feeling on top of things and comfortable in the environment we are in can reduce stress and overwhelm and let us focus on the things we need or want to do.

- make a plan for the day

- declutter your living space

- write a shopping list for the week

- change your bedclothes

- do some laundry

- organise your shelves

- set your intentions for the day (see page 192-4)

- make a list of tasks you need to do.

Add some of your own ideas for focusing on hygiene and order

* . . . .

* . . . .

* . . . .

* . . . .

* . . . .

* . . . .

USE THIS SPACE TO WRITE DOWN SOME IDEAS FOR SELF-CARE YOU WOULD LIKE TO TRY IN THE SHORT TERM:

* ....

* ....

* ....

* ....

* ....

* ....

USE THIS SPACE TO WRITE DOWN SOME IDEAS FOR SELF-CARE YOU WOULD LIKE TO PRIORITISE IN THE LONG TERM:

* ....

* ....

* ....

* ....

* ....

Mindfulness and self-care are practices, not a quick fix

' In my work with young LGBTQ+ people, and also my volunteering with Samaritans, I have noticed that although there is more awareness of mental-health issues nowadays, self-compassion can be lacking, and people are often after a quick fix. I recommend mindfulness quite a lot, but it's important to understand what it is, what you need to do to get it to work and how it can help. Meditation apps are marketed or prescribed as a 'get better quick' tool, but this perception that you can 'go and do a mindfulness' is kind of misleading. If someone's mind is going at a million miles an hour, they don't want to lie down and breathe and listen to those thoughts: they are actively trying *not* to think about what's going on for them. Then, if they do eventually sit down and do a mindfulness session and it doesn't fix anything right away, they beat themselves up, or believe it's not working. But being mindful is just the beginning. If you start a meditative practice, you have to be aware that it might be difficult at the start, that you won't be able to do it right the first time, and that's OK. You need to be in the right frame of mind, and you must recognise that your brain is a muscle, and this is a practice – you need to do it regularly to feel any effect. This is not a quick-fix solution that you can do on your phone and then feel better.

We also need to practise self-compassion – treating ourselves with empathy, understanding and kindness. One of the best ways to do this is through self-care. It's not just about being in the here and now, it's about laying the foundations for a practice that's there to support you when you need it. Sometimes it's spending the evening having a bath and watching your favourite TV show, and sometimes it's putting on that load of laundry and doing five minutes of mindfulness practice. This provides the necessary distraction in the moment when you are feeling bad, particularly if your thoughts are out of control. But self-care is also about asking yourself compassionately, 'Is the tomorrow version of me going to be grateful for what I did today?'

It's also about those days when you have a million things to think about and you're running the treadmill of the daily grind. In those moments you won't be thinking about putting together your personal crisis plan (pages 16-17) or noting down your coping mechanisms to remind yourself that this is something you can get through. That is why it's so essential we carve out time to practise coping techniques while we're in a calm state or a good place, so that when we *are* struggling, reaching for them feels like second nature. It's an ongoing practice, in the same way that you wouldn't go out for one walk and instantly feel fitter. But if you go out for a walk every day, you will begin to see an improvement in your fitness over time. Set yourself an easy goal to start. Just a few minutes of mindfulness a few times a week, building it up as you become more confident.

Just like therapy, some types of self-care won't make you feel better immediately, and they might even unearth some things that you need to spend more time working on. Put in the work now so you have the tools to help you when things get tough. It's hard work to begin with, and you might be nervous about putting in all that effort when you won't feel the effects immediately. You might be nervous about showing up because you don't want to face what's going on. But even if it's challenging, or you feel you've not quite got it right, remember that this is about helping you feel and cope better in the long run.

— **Sarah, Samaritans Cymru**

TRY TO DRAW WHAT YOUR THOUGHTS AND FEELINGS LOOK LIKE

When I'm in a calm state, my thoughts look like...
For example, this could be a shape, or a line, or absolutely anything you like.

When I'm in a state of stress/anxiety/overwhelm, my thoughts look like...
For example, this could be a scribble or a cloud – you can draw anything that you think of.

Positive affirmations

Use this space to learn or write some affirmations that can help train your brain to think in a more positive way. Here are some you might wish to learn off by heart:

• I matter.

• I am enough.

• I accept myself.

• I am here. It is now.

• Every day is a new start.

• It's OK to feel the way I feel.

• This feels hard, but I've got through it before.

Use this space to write some of your own affirmations for a positive mindset:

* . . . .

* . . . .

* . . . .

* . . . .

* . . . .

* . . . .

Your wellbeing toolbox

It can be hard to cope when you're facing something emotionally difficult. But what's important is having a toolbox that is personal to you.
Fill it with the things that work best with your patterns of behaviour
and that you know will be most helpful to you in a difficult, upsetting
or distressing situation.

You need a good balance in your toolbox of the 'softer' elements of self-care
as well as the tools that you will use constantly. Think about things that
work best for you, whether that's exercise, mindfulness, crafting, building
relationships, reaching out to friends – all the things you will come back
to time and time again that are really going to help you in the long term.
Then address potential crisis moments – if things feel really tough, you
might not want to sit down and meditate, but perhaps having a warm
bubble bath will help calm you right then and there, in that moment. Try
to identify the things that will help when you're feeling bad as well as
acknowledging the things you might need to work on for your long-term
wellbeing. What is the superglue that will hold you together, or the WD40
that will loosen you up when you need to ask for help and support?

Asking for practical support

Sometimes, when you are going through a hard time, you might want to ask someone for help with practical tasks like cooking, washing or other daily chores. It can be hard to vocalise what you are going through. Often, when you are really suffering emotionally, you might feel like it doesn't matter what anyone says – that in that moment, nothing can make you feel better. At these times, just having someone there can make all the difference. Don't be afraid to ask for help with practical tasks to take some of the weight off your shoulders.

Here are a few ideas for things you might ask for help with:

- buying and preparing food

- sorting out bills

- getting up and dressed

- getting a lift somewhere

- looking after your pet

- completing household chores

- dealing with other practical tasks.

Keeping on top of the practical things that need to be done day-to-day might stop you from feeling overwhelmed and anxious. Use this space to write notes for a possible to-do list that you could share with someone when you are struggling:

To-do list

* . . . .

* . . . .

* . . . .

* . . . .

Self check-in

What are you thinking?

. . . .

What are you feeling?

. . . .

Can you accept your thoughts and feelings without judgement?

. . . .

Can you put a name to your emotions?

. . . .

Can you accept these emotions without self-judgement?

. . . .

Do you believe that this will pass?

. . . .

When the worst of the feelings are gone, can you recognise why you felt that way?

. . . .

Can you understand what made you feel the way you did?

. . . .

Can you let go of trying to control your emotions, even when you're worried that this thought or feeling might happen again?

. . . .

What are your coping mechanisms?

. . . .

What will you do next time this thought or feeling surfaces?

. . . .

SELF-SOOTHING

When I feel . . . ., these are the things that make
me feel better:

. . . .

. . . .

. . . .

When I feel . . . ., these are the things that make
me feel better:

. . . .

. . . .

. . . .

When I feel . . . ., these are the things that make
me feel better:

. . . .

. . . .

. . . .

When I feel . . . ., these are the things that make
me feel better:

. . . .

. . . .

COLOUR BREATHING

When you experience negative thoughts, feelings or emotions, imagine your body is being filled with a certain colour – purple, for example, although you can choose any colour you like.

To get rid of the negative energy in your body, imagine that the air you're breathing in is a different colour – yellow, for example, although it can be any colour you have positive associations with.

To make more space for the yellow colour, you need to breathe out the purple colour. Keep breathing in for a certain count – in for four and out for six is an easy one to remember – and keep focusing on increasing the positive colour until it has completely taken over from the negative colour.

What do you notice when you breathe in?

. . . .

. . . .

. . . .

. . . .

What do you notice when you breathe out?

. . . .

. . . .

. . . .

. . . .

'No act of kindness however small,
is ever wasted'

– AESOP

I HAVE HELPED OTHERS BY...

. . . .

. . . .

. . . .

. . . .

I CAN HELP OTHERS BY...

. . . .

. . . .

. . . .

. . . .

I HAVE MADE OTHERS HAPPY BY...

. . . .

. . . .

I WILL MAKE OTHERS HAPPY BY...

. . . .

. . . .

. . . .

. . . .

I am grateful

Write what you are into the sun's rays, for example, 'I am grateful.'

* . . . .

* . . . .

* . . . .

* . . . .

* . . . .

'Seek the path that demands
your whole being'

– RUMI

Chapter 10
Over to you

The final pages of this journal contain some prompts for reflections and setting intentions, and mood-tracker templates to help you keep track of the way you're feeling.

At the end of a conversation with a Samaritan, people often say, 'Thank you so much for your amazing advice.' Of course, giving advice isn't something we do – we've simply listened and helped that person formulate their thoughts in a way that has allowed them to get a little clarity and move into a slightly better headspace. So, I always want to say, 'Remember to give *yourself* the credit! The journey began with you. The person helping you along and bearing a portion of the weight for one small part of the journey alleviated the burden, but they did it because they listened to what *you* were telling them. And then *you* made the decision that was right for you in that moment.'

It's the same here. Whatever you want to do next – whether that's making a promise to yourself to build a practice of good self-reflection, deciding to research more about the different aspects of emotional well-being, choosing to prioritise self-care, or planning to talk through the contents of this journal with someone – all of this is good if it feels good to you.

Take care on whichever path you choose, and remember that you never need to be alone with your thoughts and feelings – there is always someone here to listen.

END-OF-DAY REFLECTION

Date: . . . . /. . . . . /. . . . .

What have you done well today?

. . . .

. . . .

. . . .

How will you congratulate yourself?

. . . .

. . . .

. . . .

SET YOUR INTENTIONS FOR THE DAY AHEAD

Date: . . . . /. . . . . /. . . . .

Today I would like to focus on...

. . . .

. . . .

. . . .

My daily routine will be...

. . . .

. . . .

. . . .

Today I will show kindness to myself by...

. . . .

. . . .

. . . .

Today I will show kindness to others by...

. . . .

. . . .

. . . .

Today I will...
For example: listen to myself, prioritise time to connect with myself, connect with someone else, use self-compassion and not judge myself, not judge anyone else.

. . . .

. . . .

. . . .

Today I will practise self-care by...

. . . .

. . . .

. . . .

Today I will practise self-compassion by...

. . . .

. . . .

. . . .

Today I will practise self-empathy by...

. . . .

. . . .

. . . .

Today I will reward myself for everything I have achieved by...

. . . .

. . . .

. . . .

SET YOUR INTENTIONS FOR THE WEEK AHEAD

Date: . . . . / . . . . / . . . .

This week I would like to focus on...

. . . .

. . . .

. . . .

My weekly routine will include...

. . . .

. . . .

. . . .

This week I will show kindness to myself by...

. . . .

. . . .

. . . .

This week I will show kindness to others by...

. . . .

. . . .

. . . .

This week I will...

. . . .

. . . .

. . . .

This week I will practise self-care by...

. . . .

. . . .

. . . .

This week I will practise self-compassion by...

. . . .

. . . .

. . . .

This week I will practise self-empathy by...

. . . .

. . . .

. . . .

This week I will reward myself for everything I have achieved by...

. . . .

Daily mood-tracker

Use this page to make a note of your feelings and see if there are any patterns you might like to reflect on. Be aware that you might not always feel the effects of your actions today, so try and track how you feel and then look at what you've recorded. Ask yourself what you might be able to do today that would enable you to do a little more tomorrow – whatever your goal might be, however big or small.

In the chart below, fill in the feelings you would like to track – choose whatever will be most helpful to you. The first two are filled in as examples. Each day, just mark the box that best represents your feelings for that day.

Week commencing: . . . . / . . . . / . . . .

Today, I felt...

	Mon	Tues	Wed	Thurs	Fri	Sat	Sun
Happy							
Sad							

Use this space for any additional notes and reflections:

On Monday, I...

. . . .

On Tuesday, I...

. . . .

On Wednesday, I...

. . . .

On Thursday, I...

. . . .

On Friday, I...

. . . .

On Saturday, I...

. . . .

On Sunday, I...

. . . .

Weekly self-care checklist

Make a list of all the things you'd like to do as part of your self-care routine. If you need a reminder of ideas, head back to pages 162-74. Try and tick off at least one of them each day, to get into the habit of making the time to treat yourself with kindness and compassion. For each point on the list, as you are doing it, remind yourself of the importance of self-care, and focus on connecting with the present moment. Write down a few lines of reflection for each day.

Week commencing: . . . ./. . . . ./. . . . .

	Mon	Tues	Wed	Thurs	Fri	Sat	Sun
Drink some water							
Practise some breathing exercises							
Go outside for some fresh air							

Weekly mood-tracker

Use this space for a more general reflection about how you're feeling over a longer period of time. If you find that your emotions, thoughts and behaviours fluctuate on more of a day-to-day basis, you might prefer to use the daily mood-tracker on the previous pages. But sometimes, when we've gone through a big life change, or a period of significant upheaval, it can be really helpful to look back over that time and see how far you've come, or if there's a pattern of behaviour in which you've got stuck and might need a little help in changing.

Write some general feelings that you'd like to focus on in the first column – perhaps make them a little less specific than the things you're tracking with the daily mood-tracker. The first three have been filled in as an example. Each week, mark the box that best represents your overall feelings for that week.

Date that I began tracking: . . . . / . . . . / . . . .

	Week 1	Week 2	Week 3	Week 4	Week 5	Week 6
Good						
Not great						
Up and down						

	Week 7	Week 8	Week 9	Week 10	Week 11	Week 12
Good						
Not great						
Up and down						

	Week 13	Week 14	Week 15	Week 16	Week 17	Week 18
Good						
Not great						
Up and down						

My reflections on the pattern of my moods over a period of weeks:

. . . .

My to-do list

Remember to make the first thing on your list 'make a list': that way, you will always be always to tick at least one thing off.

Date: ..../............/............

* ....

* ....

* ....

* ....

* ....

* ....

Where to seek further support

You can get in touch with Samaritans to talk about anything that's troubling you, no matter how large or small the issue feels. You can get free, confidential emotional support at any time by calling our 24-hour listening service on 116 123, or emailing us at jo@samaritans.org. The number won't show up on your bill. Please also visit www.samaritans.org for more information about our services.

If you're looking for advice or specialist support for a particular issue, these organisations may be able to help.

ADDICTION

Alcoholics Anonymous
For anyone with a desire to tackle their own drink problem.
alcoholics-anonymous.org.uk

Al-Anon
Offers understanding and support for families and friends of problem-drinkers in an anonymous environment, whether the alcoholic is still drinking or not.
Tel: 0800 0086 811
www.al-anonuk.org.uk
Tel: 01 873 2699 (Republic of Ireland)
al-anon-ireland.org (Republic of Ireland)

Dan 24/7 (Wales)
Support with drug and alcohol problems.
Tel: 0808 808 2234
Text: 81066
dan247.org.uk

Drinkline
UK-wide helpline for anyone concerned about their alcohol use or someone else's.
Tel: 0300 123 1110
drinkaware.co.uk/alcohol-support-services

Drugs.ie (Republic of Ireland)
Provides support, information, guidance and referral to anyone with a question or concern related to drug and alcohol use and/or HIV and sexual health.
Tel: 1800 459 459 (Freephone)
drugs.ie

Dunlewey Addiction Services (Northern Ireland)
Confidential counselling and mentoring programme for those experiencing difficulties with their own, or other people's substance misuse or gambling issues.
Tel: 028 9039 2547
Tel: 0800 886 725
dunlewey.net

Frank
Friendly, confidential drugs advice.
Tel: 0300 123 6600
Text: 82111
talktofrank.com

Gamblers Anonymous
Group meeting support at locations around the country for those who wish to recover from gambling addiction.
Tel: 0330 094 0322
gamblersanonymous.org.uk
Tel: 01 872 1133 (Republic of Ireland)
gamblersanonymous.ie (Republic of Ireland)

GamCare
Information, advice, support and free counselling for the prevention and treatment of problem gambling.
Tel: 0808 802 0133
gamcare.org.uk

Know the Score (Scotland)
Free, confidential information about drugs.
Tel: 0333 230 9468
gamcare.org.uk

BENEFITS AND RIGHTS

Citizens Advice
Impartial advice on rights and responsibilities across the UK.
Tel: 0344 411 1444 (England and Wales)
Tel: 0808 800 9060 (Scotland)
Tel: 0344 477 2020 (Welsh Speaker)
Tel: 0800 028 1881 (Northern Ireland)
citizensadvice.org.uk

Farming Community Network
Confidential help and advice to those within the farming community.
Tel: 0300 011 1999
Email: help@fcn.org.uk
fcn.org.uk

BEREAVEMENT

Child Bereavement UK
Support for families when a baby or child of any age dies or is dying, or when a child is facing bereavement.
Tel: 0800 028 8840
Email: support@childbereavementuk.org
childbereavementuk.org

Cruse (England/Scotland)
Offers support for bereaved people. Also supports those coping with the death of pets.
Tel: 0808 808 1677
Tel: 0845 600 2227 (Cruse Scotland)
Email: helpline@cruse.org.uk
cruse.org.uk
crusescotland.org.uk (Cruse Scotland)

The Irish Hospice Foundation (Republic of Ireland)
Offers information and resources to support bereaved persons. Website provides info re: Covid-19, including funeral information.
Tel: 01 679 3188
hospicefoundation.ie/bereavement

CARERS

Carers UK
Support for unpaid carers for family or friends.
Tel: 0808 808 7777 (England, Scotland, Wales)
Tel: 028 9043 9843 (Northern Ireland)
Email: advice@carersuk.org
carersuk.org

Family Action (England and Wales)
Provides emotional and practical support around family pressures.
Tel: 0808 802 6666
Text: 07537 404 282
Email: familyline@family-action.org.uk
family-action.org.uk

Family Carers Ireland (Republic of Ireland)
The Carers Association provides a number of services to family carers that are aimed at helping to increase the quality of life for the carer and the person receiving care at home.
Tel: 1800 240 724
familycarers.ie

CHILDREN AND YOUNG PEOPLE

ChildLine (18 years and younger)
Free help and support for children and young people in the UK.
Tel: 0800 11 11
childline.org.uk

ChildLine (Republic of Ireland)
Part of the ISPCC (The Irish Society for the Prevention of Cruelty to Children).
Tel: 1800 666 666 (under-18s only; freephone)
Tel: 01 676 7960 (parents can ring)
Text: 50101 (free text)
childline.ie

Jigsaw (Republic of Ireland)
Jigsaw strives to ensure that no young person feels alone, isolated or disconnected from others around them by providing vital support to young people with their mental health and working closely with communities across Ireland.
Tel: 01 4727 010
jigsaw.ie

The Mix
Free help and support for children and young people aged 25 years and younger in the UK.
Tel: 0808 808 4994
themix.org.uk

CRISIS PREGNANCY

Positive Options (Republic of Ireland)
State-funded organisation that offers a range of crisis pregnancy counselling services to women with a crisis pregnancy and their partners.
Tel: 1800 828 010
Text: 50444 (free text list)
positiveoptions.ie

Pregnancy Crisis Helpline
The Pregnancy Crisis Helpline offers you a safe, confidential place for you to talk about your unplanned pregnancy or previous abortion.
Tel: 0800 368 9296
pregnancycrisishelpline.org.uk

DEBT, POVERTY AND SOCIAL INCLUSION

Citizens Information Board (Republic of Ireland)
Statutory body that supports the provision of information, advice and advocacy on a broad range of public and social services.
Tel: 0761 07 4000
citizensinformation.ie

MABS – Money Advice and Budgeting Service (Republic of Ireland)
A national free, confidential and independent service for people in debt or in danger of getting into debt.
Tel: 0761 07 2000
mabs.ie

Society of St Vincent de Paul
Exists to fight poverty. Their network gives practical support to those experiencing poverty and social exclusion by providing a wide range of services to those in need.
Tel: 07587 035 121
svp.org.uk
Tel: 01 884 8200 (Republic of Ireland)
svp.ie (Republic of Ireland)

Step Change Debt Charity
Comprehensive debt advice for people in the UK.
Tel: 0800 138 1111
stepchange.org

EATING DISORDERS

Anorexia Bulimia Care
Personal care and support for anyone affected by anorexia, bulimia, binge-eating and all types of eating distress.
Tel: 00300 011 1213
anorexiabulimiacare.org.uk

Beat
Support and information relating to eating disorders.
Tel: 0808 801 0677 (adults over 18)
Email: help@beateatingdisorders.org.uk (adults over 18)
Tel: 0808 801 0711 (youth line – under 18)
Email: fyp@beateatingdisorders.org.uk (youth line – under 18)
beateatingdisorders.org.uk

Bodywhys (Republic of Ireland)
Provides a range of support services for people affected by eating disorders, including specific services for families and friends.
Tel: 01 210 7906 (Lo-call number)
Email: alex@bodywhys.ie
bodywhys.ie

HEALTH

NHS 111 (England, Northern Ireland, Wales and Scotland)
Health advice and reassurance.
Tel: 111
111.nhs.ukhse.ie (Republic of Ireland)

HOUSING AND HOMELESSNESS

Shelter (England, Scotland and Wales) / Housing Rights (Northern Ireland)
Housing and homelessness charity offering advice and information.
Tel: 0808 800 4444 (England, Scotland)
Tel: 08000 495 495 (Wales)
Tel: 028 9024 5640 (Northern Ireland)
shelter.org.uk

Threshold (Republic of Ireland)
National charity providing independent advisory and advocacy services, working in collaboration with others for those disadvantaged by the housing system. Their aim is to provide long-term solutions for people who are homeless.
Tel: 1800 454 454
threshold.ie

LONELINESS AND ISOLATION

Alone (Republic of Ireland)
Supporting older people who are socially isolated, homeless or living in poverty or crisis. They offer befriending, housing support, support coordination and assistance with technology.
Tel: 081 822 224
Email: hello@alone.ie
alone.ie

Befrienders Worldwide
International charity providing confidential support to people in emotional crisis or distress, or those close to them. It includes a directory of emotional support helplines around the world.
befrienders.org

MENTAL HEALTH

Aware (Northern Ireland)
Confidential helpline and email service for people who are experiencing depression.
Tel: 028 9035 7820 (free in Northern Ireland)
Email: help@aware-ni.org
aware-ni.org

Aware (Republic of Ireland)
The organisation undertakes to create a society where people with depression are understood and supported, are free from stigma, and have access to a broad range of appropriate therapies to enable them to reach their full potential.
Tel: 1800 804 848 (Freephone)
aware.ie

Mental Health First Aid England (MHFA)
A social enterprise offering expert guidance and training to support mental health in the workplace and beyond.
mhfaengland.org
mhfaireland.ie

SAMH (Scotland)
Mental health information and signposting to local services. (Not a listening service or suitable for people in crisis.)
Tel: 0141 530 1000
Email: enquire@samh.org.uk
samh.org.uk

MILITARY

Veterans' Gateway
Veterans' Gateway is the first point of contact for veterans/military personnel and families seeking support.
Tel: 0808 802 1212
Text: 81212
veteransgateway.org.uk

OLDER PEOPLE

Age UK
Support for older people.
Tel: 0800 679 1602 (England)
Tel: 0800 022 3444 (Wales)
Tel: 0800 124 4222* (Scotland)
Tel: 0808 808 7575 (Northern Ireland)
ageuk.org.uk
* Age Scotland operates its helpline in
partnership with The Silver Line.

The Silver Line
Information, friendship and advice for older people.
Tel: 0800 470 80 90
thesilverline.org.uk

RELATIONSHIPS

Relate
Counselling and workshops on relationships and family issues.
Tel: 0300 100 1234 (Relate)
Tel: 028 9032 3454 (Relate NI)
Webchat available (check website)
relate.org.uk

Relationships Scotland
Counselling, family mediation and child contact centres.
Tel: 0345 119 2020
relationships-scotland.org.uk

SEXUALITY

Switchboard, the LGBT+ helpline
A safe space for anyone to discuss sexuality, gender identity, sexual health and emotional wellbeing.
Tel: 0300 330 0630
Email: chris@switchboard.lgbt
switchboard.lgbt

LGBT (Republic of Ireland)
Supporting lesbian, gay, bisexual and transgender people and their families.
Tel: 1890 929 539
lgbt.ie

SEXUAL/DOMESTIC ABUSE

Men's Aid (Republic of Ireland) – men only
National service for men experiencing domestic violence in Ireland, supplying support and information.
Tel: 01 554 3811
Email: hello@mensaid.ie
mensaid.ie

Men's Advice Line – men only
Confidential helpline for men experiencing domestic violence in any relationship.
Tel: 0808 801 0327
Email: info@mensadviceline.org.uk
mensadviceline.org.uk

NAPAC (National Association for People Abused in Childhood)
Offers support to adult (18+) survivors of all types of childhood abuse.
Tel: 0800 801 0331
napac.org.uk

Rape Crisis (England, Wales, Scotland and Northern Ireland) – women only
Tel: 0808 802 9999 (England and Wales) –
12pm–2.30 p.m. and 7–9.30 p.m. every day,
plus 3–5.30 p.m. on weekdays
Tel: 0808 801 0302 (Scotland) – 6 p.m.–
midnight daily
Tel: 1800 778 888 (Northern Ireland) –
24-hour helpline
rapecrisis.org.uk

Rape Crisis Centre (Republic of Ireland)
Takes calls from women and men of all ages who have experienced or want to talk about the effects of any kind of sexual violence.
Tel: 1800 778 888
drcc.ie

Refuge National Domestic Violence Helpline – women only
Support for women experiencing domestic violence (including forced marriages, tech abuse and modern slavery).
Tel: 0808 200 0247
www.nationaldomesticviolencehelpline.org.uk

Women's Aid (Republic of Ireland)
Committed to the elimination of violence and abuse of women through effecting political, cultural and social change. Women's Aid provides direct support services to women experiencing male violence and abuse.
Tel: 1800 341 900
www.womensaid.ie

TALKING THERAPIES

BACP (British Association for Counselling and Psychotherapy)
BACP is a membership organisation that sets standards for therapeutic practice. Their online directory can be used to locate a professional counsellor, who will usually charge for their services.
Tel: 01455 883300
Email: bacp@bacp.co.uk
bacp.co.uk

Connect Counselling (Republic of Ireland)
Counselling service for any adult who has experienced abuse, trauma or neglect in childhood. The service is also available to partners or relatives of people with these experiences.
Tel: 1800 477 477
connectcounselling.ie

GROW (Republic of Ireland)
A mental-health organisation that helps people who have suffered, or are suffering, from mental health problems.
Tel: 1890 474 474
grow.ie

Mind (England and Wales)
Advice, support and information around mental-health issues. Mind has a legal-advice line in England and Wales.
Tel: 0300 123 3393
Text: 86463
Email: info@mind.org.uk
mind.org.uk

Pieta House (Republic of Ireland)
Provides a specialised treatment programme for people who have suicidal ideation or who engage in self-harming behaviours. They also provide support and help to people bereaved by suicide.
Tel: 1800 247 247
pieta.ie

Shine (Republic of Ireland)
National organisation dedicated to upholding the rights and addressing the needs of all those affected by enduring mental illness including, but not exclusively, schizophrenia, schizo-affective disorder and bipolar disorder, through the promotion and provision of high-quality services.
shine.ie

Shout
Free 24/7 text service support for anyone in crisis and struggling to cope.
Text: 85258
giveusashout.org

UKCP (UK Council for Psychotherapy)
The leading body for the training and accreditation of psychotherapists and psychotherapeutic counsellors in the UK. UKCP has over 10,000 members helping to improve lives through support to mental health and emotional wellbeing, both privately and through the NHS and charitable partnerships.
psychotherapy.co.uk

VICTIMS OF CRIME

Crime Victim's Helpline (Republic of Ireland)
Confidential support to victims of crime.
Tel: 116006
crimevictimshelpline.ie

Victim Support
Help for victims of crime, witnesses and their families and friends.
Tel: 0808 168 9111 (England and Wales)
Tel: 0800 160 1985 (Scotland)
Tel: 028 9024 3133 (Northern Ireland)
victimsupport.org.uk